A Concise Guide to Navigating
Artificial Intelligence
for Writers and Publishers

The

Revolution
in Book Publishing

A Concise Guide to Navigating
Artificial Intelligence
for Writers and Publishers

The

AI

Revolution
in Book Publishing

Thad McIlroy

The AI Revolution in Book Publishing

A Concise Guide to Navigating Artificial Intelligence for Writers and Publishers

English Edition Print ISBN: 978-0-9813608-5-0
English Edition PDF ISBN: 978-0-9813608-7-4
English Edition EPUB ISBN: 978-0-9813608-6-7

Contents

Introduction

"The next revolution will catch us all off guard, as they always do. Said another way: if the crowd is anticipating the revolution, it can't be the revolution." —Doc Searls, 2002

It's been two-and-a-half years since OpenAI introduced ChatGPT to a public mostly unfamiliar with artificial intelligence. Initially it appeared to have no obvious relevance to book publishing. Since then, everything has changed. And nothing has changed. Publishers are now delving into the new AI tools, exploring the edges, and engaging in chats with ChatGPT. But there's no sign of a true revolution in the practice of publishing; it's just too soon.

There is an abundance of uncertainty around AI's role in writing and publishing. Major controversies and concerns surround AI's use. Still, for many, there's excitement about the possibilities.

I'm going to focus here more on promise than on peril. But I do include an overview on the concerns and risks surrounding AI, particularly as they apply to authors and publishers. I'm not seeking to belittle the concerns, many of them severely troubling. They're just not what this book is about.

Is it a book?

I consider this publication to be more of a 'booklet' than a book. The UNESCO definition of a book is "at least 49 pages" (why not 50?)[1], and, at 300 words per page, this one at one point looked like it might have failed to qualify. But, more importantly, it's not intended to be the definitive word on anything—it's more of a progress report. Artificial intelligence, and its role in book publishing, are changing at a breakneck pace, which shows no signs of slowing down. So this book(let), this report, is just a snapshot.

Using the Leanpub platform[2], I've been releasing my research and analysis as a work in progress—it's revised as a living document. I've never attempted this before. My reasons are two-fold: to offer something useful in the short-term, and to have the facility to continue to revise it as required. The AI story is far from over. (This latest version was extensively updated in May 2025.)

I hope my approach will prove useful for readers, though I'm aware that too many updates could become annoying. I've tried to reduce the *topicality* of this book, to reduce the focus on the stuff that's going to change the fastest.

The version of the book that was (quietly) available beginning in April 2024 was marked as "75% complete" and offered for free to readers. I then expanded the book to a "90% edition," also for free. July 23, 2024 was the official pub date for the "100% complete" version, which I put into wider distribution outside of Leanpub, via Amazon and the IngramSpark network. I'm continuing to update the 100% version: but most updates will only be available to Leanpub buyers—it's unwieldy to constantly update print, ebooks and audiobooks, that are in wider distribution. (I'm planning to release the May 2025 version also on Amazon et al.)

Publisher pain with AI itself

I'm hearing daily about the pain that people across the publishing industry are facing trying to come to terms with AI. Why is it so painful? Here are three possible reasons:

- The technology is complex and mysterious, too complex for non-scientists to understand. Anxiety is common. (There's a fascinating study[3] positing an "AI anxiety scale (AIAS)" measuring 21 different reasons that people are anxious about AI.)
- AI has become vastly controversial in publishing, mainly because of copyright issues that strike at the heart of authoring and publishing.
- Yet there's also an atmosphere of FOMO—Fear Of Missing Out. Despite AI's many flaws, as with other alluring technologies (the Apple watch? Blockchain/Bitcoin?), we face that gnawing feeling: what if I'm missing out on the *next* big thing, like I did on a couple of the last really big things. I felt stupid then; I don't want to feel stupid again.

All right: It makes sense that publishing people are feeling some AI pain.

So what then is the use case for this book?

The use case is that you work in book publishing, or you're an author trying to better understand book publishing, and you're sick of feeling stupid and confused around AI. Too many of your colleagues appear to understand it better than you do, and you're tired of not being able to engage intelligently on the topic.

My goal for readers is that, by the end of this book, they'll feel enabled to join the conversation, to express an informed opinion. I want you to feel equipped to make personal choices around the technology, and have a path for learning more about how to use AI, if you choose to do so.

I *do not* want to inundate readers with lots of blah-blah about the underpinnings of AI technology—I'm not going to talk much about AI in the abstract. Instead, I want to give you a grounding in AI specifically for book authoring and publishing. If someone asks you, what does natural language processing *really* mean, you can answer, as I do: I'm not an AI expert. But I do know how AI is being used in my industry.

Will it be just what you need to know?

I dislike the phrase "what you need to know" because it so rarely lives up to its billing, often missing wide of the mark, either far more than you need to know, or far less. Will I get it right? I'm serious about trying to convey the minimum. I think I know what publishers need to know about AI, as I've been talking to lots of them, while hosting seminars and webinars designed very specifically to provide just the basics.

Rather than endlessly repeating the phrase "what you need to know" I'll use a key logo with some indented text.

After the summaries that introduce most sections, I'll expand on the main concepts. I've also kept these as short as possible, though, truth be told, sometimes I do go on.

A short-form I'm going to use is "Chat AI." When OpenAI first released ChatGPT, it was the only kid on the block, but now there are a half-dozen important competitors. I'll go into the specifics shortly, but you've heard of some of them already, from Google and from Microsoft. They (and several other companies) now offer online AI chat software that's similar to ChatGPT. And so rather than saying "ChatGPT and its competitors" I'll just refer to the whole category as "Chat AI." If I write "ChatGPT" I'll be referring specifically to OpenAI's software.

The book is mostly practical, but in the final section I posit an essay on what may be the real-world consequences of AI on the book publishing industry, alongside a few other conjectural spinnings.

Who is this book for?

The primary audience for this book is trade (consumer) book publishers. A secondary audience is all other book publishers (scholarly, educational...) to the extent that there are overlaps in these industry sectors, and in their approach to using AI in their workflows.

The subtitle states this is a guide to AI for both writers and publishers. Authors are an important audience for me. In part that's because I want publishers to understand what writers are doing with this technology. I think that's important. At its 2024 annual meeting, the BISG (the Book Industry Study Group), which mostly represents trade publishers, indicated that "it is looking to draw from a broader pool including, literary agents and authors."[4] That's a welcome move.

I want writers to read this book because it can help them understand what publishers are doing with their manuscripts. Self-published authors always keep one eye on traditional publishing—they are, de facto, publishers themselves—and so the AI technology of interest to publishers will be of interest to them.

But, make no mistake, this is *not* a hands-on how-to for authors on using AI to be better and more productive writers. There are numerous books on that topic (sadly, many of them just scammy Amazon rip-offs). And lots of YouTube videos (of varying quality).

Within trade book publishing my ideal reader is not necessarily a decision-maker, but rather one of the many people who work across the industry every day, creating books and finding readers. I'll be talking about all of the key publishing functions in this book, from editorial through to sales and distribution. And about the intersection of writers with readers.

Though I grew up in Canada, and began my publishing career there, I'm based in San Francisco, in the United States, and so I default to thinking about the U.S. publishing industry. But just about everything in this booklet should be as relevant to a publisher in Madagascar as it is to a publisher in Manhattan. While publishers in smaller countries face challenges of scale, so do small publishers in America, and this book is intended for companies of all sizes.

When I talk to small publishers about AI, and when I talk to very large publishers about AI, the big difference that I notice is the notion of the publishing 'enterprise.' The largest publishers are often part of (or adjacent to) public companies, and once you're a public company, issues around reputation and security loom so much larger than they do for an everyday publisher, not accountable in the same way to shareholders and the news media. While an editor at a Big 5 publisher has the same use for AI tools as a freelance editor working for smaller outfits, the context in which they use the tools is quite different.

How much do you need to know about AI to read this book?

I'm assuming that my audience has roughly zero knowledge about AI's innards, but that they're smart readers. So I'll be treading that fine line between zero knowledge, and not talking down to readers.

I do imagine that just about everyone has heard about the new generation of AI: a YouGov poll, in January 2025, suggests that only 7% of Americans know "nothing at all" about AI. Writers and publishers have almost certainly heard about some of the copyright complaints, but probably don't have a grasp of the issues. So I don't have to explain that AI stands for "Artificial Intelligence." But I won't assume readers can define what AI is, what it means, its potential impact, and so on. That's why you're here.

Accessibility, both broadly and specifically

My mantra for the publication of this book is 'accessibility.'

For most people, that merely means something akin to 'availability,' and, indeed, I intend to make this book available in as many forms and formats as I can conceive of. I want to expand the concept of the bookish container. I'm trying to make my book an exemplary publication, highlighting the full range of what can be achieved today when publishing a single book.

On Leanpub you'll find the book available as a PDF file, an EPUB file, and as a free-of-charge web-based publication. You'll find translations into 31 languages, including the major Asian and European languages. There will be multiple audiobooks in major languages—so far I've got French and German; more to follow.

I also make the book available, in print and digital formats, on all the ecommerce platforms that can be accessed via Ingram and Amazon. That includes most of the book online retail sites, in much of the world. And this way libraries will also be able to buy the book, though, understandably, they have slight space available for self-published work. (I'm happy to donate digital copies to any library in the world that requests one, or to provide a print copy at cost.)

It doesn't make sense to record a video of the entire book, when audiobooks are available. But some people prefer to access content via video. So I'll offer abridged video versions, in multiple lengths.

And what about the human touch? I've also been available via webinars or one-on-one online consultations, via my website and blog. I can even be hired to show up in person!

'Accessibility' means much more than its dictionary definition. As the folks at the Canadian National Network for Equitable Library Service (NNELS) put it[5], "An accessible book is one that can be used and understood by everyone." And so my English EPUB file meets the W3C 1.1 recommendation[6] for the print-disabled, including robust alt text[7] descriptions for images. We hope to meet this accessibility standard for the foreign language translations as well.

The alt-text was created with ChatGPT. I didn't edit ChatGPT's version, so that anyone reading the EPUB can see how good it is, and where it's still lacking. As my colleague Bill Kasdorf reminds me, good alt-text describes what a sighted reader derives from an image, not just what the image *appears* to be.

For book publishers, accessibility is no longer an option: it's a default setting.

(I have two *mea culpas* to share: Because of limitations within the publishing platforms, the default PDF file will unfortunately not meet the PDF/UA spec, nor will I be able to offer a large print version of the book on ecommerce sites.)

Some housekeeping

As indicated, this book is (relatively) short. When you call a short-ish document 'a book' you run the risk of buyers protesting, "I thought I was buying a book, but it's only 50 pages long!" I've done everything I can to make it clear on the sales page that this is not a full-length book, but if you're disappointed, keep in mind that Leanpub offers a 60-day money-back guarantee, and I'll happily extend that refund offer to 'forever.' I want readers to be delighted, not disappointed. (If you bought the book on another platform, email me: I'll send a check!)

The book is heavily hyperlinked (these appear in different ways in different formats, but often as footnotes). I've always believed in linking to original sources in my work, so that readers can verify my sometimes grand claims. But I'm aware that hyperlinks and footnotes can be distracting, particularly if you're using an e-reading device. I apologize for that. The best bet is to ignore the links as you read, and return to them if you want to go deeper on a topic.

I don't know in which format you're reading (or listening to) right now. Nor in which language. I've tried to make the "ergonomics" of the book as user-friendly as possible, and links and footnotes are not always optimal from that perspective.

This book has sponsors, something that I know is unusual for 'a book.' I explain how the sponsorship works in my 'disclosures' section at the end of the text.

Why AI Now?

 When I talk to publishers I hear of pressing, immediate concerns. And AI is usually not one of them.

The rising cost of print manufacturing has been vexing for several years, though it now appears to be levelling. Increased distribution costs are challenging for all players. These lead to pricing pressures—there's evidence that readers are beginning to chafe at rising prices for new hardcovers and trade paperbacks. I classify these as 'analog' problems—digital technologies bring little to the table to address them.

Then there are the broader 'existential' problems that are of ever-increasing concern, but they are inchoate issues, without obvious solutions. Included here are:

- Content discovery and audience engagement via online and social media.
- Changing consumer behavior and reading habits.
- Competition from other digital media.

I believe that AI could be tremendously helpful to publishers in these areas, but the methods are non-obvious and will take time to implement. I'll address this in later chapters of the book.

AI: Getting Started

Before I get into the boring technical background, I invite you just to jump right into the online software. The top tools are free to play with. There's ChatGPT[8]. And Claude.ai[9]. You can dally with Microsoft Copilot[10]. Or try Google's Gemini[11]. Perplexity.ai has taken the lead in AI search. It is said that Elon Musk has some AI chat tech attached to X. I've not explored this.

That's how most people start with AI—I bet you've already tried one or more of these toys. I also bet that you haven't tried them for very long. Most people I talk to devote just a few minutes. They try a few questions, get back some pretty obvious answers, and they move on.

Wrong approach.

I side with Ethan Mollick, whose work I'll describe a few times in this book. In his blog and in a recent interview[12], Mollick talks about his '10 hour rule':

> "I want to indicate that 10 hours is as arbitrary as 10,000 steps. Like, there's no scientific basis for it. This is an observation. But it also does move you past the, I poked at this for an evening, and it moves you towards using this in a serious way. I don't know if 10 hours is the real limit, but it seems to be somewhat transformative. The key is to use it in an area where you have expertise, so you can understand what it's good or bad at, can learn the shape of its capabilities."

Another commenter[13], reviewing Mollick's recent book on AI[14], pointed out an equally-true 'rule of ten': "An hour of experimenting with these tools is worth ten hours of reading about them."

You get the idea. This is about doing, not pondering. My book is a ponderance. You need to get your hands dirty.

AI: A Very Brief History

 Until a couple of years ago, the average person heard about AI only as an abstraction, either as science fiction or as something that could beat a grandmaster at chess or the game of Go. Suddenly AI is everywhere, creating a false impression that it's new. Even the new stuff isn't exactly new. But that's a moot point. AI meant little to book publishing before ChatGPT. Now it means a lot.

Understanding the roughly 70-year development of AI can be fascinating, but it's in no way required to appreciate what's going on today.

Our World In Data does a nice job of briefly recording the history[15]—I'll leave it to them.

The current generation of AI was developed mostly over the last decade. Then, suddenly, ChatGPT appeared 'overnight' on November 30, 2022. Two months later it had 100 million monthly users, the fastest that any technology has ever moved into the consumer space (Facebook took over two years to reach 100 million users).

Why the rapid adoption? First, it's fascinating and fun. Second, it's free. Third, you don't need to buy a new device to use it. And fourth, you don't need any training to initially access ChatGPT (or its Chat AI competitors). But those same factors applied also to Facebook, so why ChatGPT?

As Arthur C. Clarke famously noted, "Any sufficiently advanced technology is indistinguishable from magic." Chat AI is magic. The experience of 'talking' in everyday language to a machine... it's magical. The experience of saying "I want an image of a book in a balloon in a cloud near the sun," and, seconds later, one appears,

... is also magical. GPT-generated images are starting to look similar in style, colorful and fanciful. So I sent a second prompt "now in a style that looks like a 15th century illustration." And so:

If I want a video of a book in a balloon in a cloud near the sun, there are over a dozen tools to choose from, and presto. And a musical soundtrack to go with the video. Well, how does this sound? It's just like magic.

For fear of seeming dismissive of AI's extraordinary

abilities by relegating it to the category of inscrutable "magic," it's fun to learn that many of the scientists responsible for the current generation of AI admit that they really don't understand exactly how it works. As a report in a spring 2024 issue of the *MIT Technology Review* noted[16], "for all its runaway success, nobody knows exactly how—-or why—-it works." Exciting, but a little scary.

Understanding AI and Some Key Terminology

 AI comes with a plethora of technology and terminology, much of it inscrutable to all but data scientists. Users of Chat AI don't require an in-depth knowledge of AI terms nor the technical concepts involved. The system's conversational nature allows intuitive interactions without specialized background knowledge of how things work. Focusing on what Chat AI can actually do is more important.

In preparing this book I've struggled with what would be the professional thing for me to do as an author of a book about AI. The conventional approach is to provide a short explanation of the science and a review of frequently-used terms.

I'm not going to do that.

I'm going to offer here a few external links to what I think are some reasonably comprehensible short descriptions of AI basics.

What's the future of AI?: McKinsey & Co. (April 2024) has a good set of explainers[17].

Likewise Gartner's *Generative AI*[18] (undated) isn't bad.

Futurepedia offers a not-bad summary of *AI Fundamentals*[19] (Published December 2024)

Having disposed of the how-to, I'm now going to introduce some terms that I do think are valuable to understand. Not because you *need* to know them to use the software. Only that this set of terms points to some key aspects of how the current generation of AI actually operates.

My use case for tackling these terms and concepts is authors and publishers who (i) want to go a level deeper on AI, for whatever reason, or (ii) want to understand the context of the current criticisms of AI, or (iii) want to contribute to strategic discussions of how their colleagues or organizations should approach AI.

In other words, this is not what you need to know, but, rather, what you might like to know. Here they are, in non-alphabetical order:

Prompts and Prompting

You can open up Chat AI software and just type in a question (very much as you do currently for a Google search). For Chat AI that's called a "prompt." But "prompting" has developed into something more elaborate, a skill-set for how to structure your AI conversations to achieve optimal results. (Much more on this below.)

Large Language Model (LLM)

Large Language Models work by analyzing huge amounts of (mostly) written material, allowing them to predict what words or sentences should come next in a conversation or a piece of writing. They don't 'understand' language in the human sense, instead processing text by breaking it down into smaller pieces (called tokens), and then converting the tokens into numbers. They process the text as numbers, regurgitating more numbers, which are then converted back into text on output. That's an overly simplified explanation of why Chat AI does not 'contain' copyrighted work: it's built with numbers that represent a vast abstraction from the underlying texts.

LLMs are trained on how language is typically used and then generate responses based on this understanding. We tend to underestimate just how predictable most language is. Chat AI can generate text that is (sometimes shockingly) similar to existing literature, but, by design, it doesn't have the capability to retrieve specific excerpts or copies of copyrighted texts. (I know, many of you have heard about the *New York Times* lawsuit against OpenAI—the *Times* was able to get ChatGPT to regurgitate some portions of previously-published articles verbatim. That was a bug that's been mostly fixed.)

I think it's important to have at least a sense of the way LLMs work with language. This article on LinkedIn[20] is about how AI handles translation, but serves as a simple primer on LLM's process. A more comprehensive "jargon free" explanation can be found here[21].

Generative AI

The most important thing to understand this term is the "generative" part. Generative AI *generates* new text.

Generative Pre-trained Transformer (GPT)

This, the nerdiest of the terminology here, describes a specific type of LLM developed by OpenAI. "Generative" indicates its ability to create text, "pre-trained" signifies that it has been trained on a large body of text data, and "transformer" references the software that it uses. Knowing what GPT stands for is helpful only so that you understand what the GPT in ChatGPT represents.

ChatGPT

ChatGPT is the software you see; GPT is what's behind the software. Users experience ChatGPT, not the GPT behind it. As noted above, ChatGPT is just one of several Chat AI online software systems, with similar functionality.

One more term that you'll encounter frequently that is unfamiliar to many is:

Corpus

The dictionary definition of corpus is "a collection of written texts" (though, in fact, it's not always text). The term is used in reference to what GPTs are trained on: vast corpuses of (mostly) text. We're told that the largest corpuses contain trillions of words. For mere mortals that's impossible to comprehend. Don't you think of

Wikipedia as enormous, containing a vast number of words? Well, there are a mere 4.5 billion words in Wikipedia—GPT-4 was trained on well over a trillion.

I think that it's important to consider this scale. Authors, understandably, are worried that the 75,000 words, plus or minus, in their book might have been sucked into a large language model. Perhaps they have (more below). But assuming this is the case, consider just how little value any one book has to the magnitude of today's large language models. It's truly insignificant. Beyond insignificant. Even 10,000 books is chump change.

AI Software: The System Heavyweights

 I listed above the four Chat AI heavyweights: ChatGPT, Claude.ai, Microsoft Copilot and Google Gemini. I should include Meta AI (called Llama), although it's used less frequently. I could also include DeepSeek from China, Mistral from France and some software that Elon Musk has apparently developed via the X platform.

They each work more or less the same and deliver somewhat similar results. So which one is best? That question takes you down a rabbit hole. It's a bit like asking which seaside town offers the best beach vacation, or which SUV is best for families. There is a huge amount of nuance in the issues and a vast amount of pride and prejudice filtering the responses.

So too with this seemingly simple but still enormously complex software. I've heard people argue that Claude has more conversational skills with language, or that ChatGPT is better with software code. Microsoft Copilot, though mostly a variation of ChatGPT, integrates well with the Microsoft software suite. Google Gemini can plug into Gmail, Google Maps and YouTube. Some of the differences are meaningful; many are slight. And they're constantly changing with each new software release.

The 'best' software won't be settled for some time now. If you experiment with enough of the available tools, you'll settle on some personal favorites.

There are two top tiers of AI software. The first is what could be called the foundational software, software like ChatGPT and its competitors (aka Chat AI). That's how most people experience AI today.

The next tier is all of the other software that provides what is essentially a window into the foundational software. Newcomers to AI chat will mostly not have encountered this software, though it is not rare or obscure. Some are familiar with Jasper (marketing software) or Perplexity (search). This software would simply not exist without ChatGPT and its brethren.

Keep in mind that mainstream software from Adobe, Microsoft, Grammarly, Zoom, at al., now incorporates AI tools, but this is different from software that's built from the ground up based on LLM interfaces. (Others like Otter (for transcriptions) predate ChatGPT but are now imbued with large language model technology.)

Below we'll look at publishing-specific software that capitalizes on generative AI's abilities.

Software Paradigms

Way back when software was code and only engineers understood how it worked. What made personal computers succeed, beyond their relatively low cost, was software that was (relatively) easy to use. We don't give much thought to all of this; it just surrounds us.

But consider, for a moment, Microsoft Word, a program that I can safely assume is used by 99% of the readers of this book. It takes about 10 minutes to show someone how to write a paragraph of text in Word. Then you can show them how to create bold text, and italics, and how to change the base font, perhaps from Calibri to Arial or Times Roman. Then, how to save the file and print the file. How to search and replace.

And then you leave them on their own.

Years later you find out that they're still formatting their Word paragraphs with spaces and tabs. And still forgetting to save their files, or getting mixed up about which version they saved, sometimes having to recreate text from scratch. But they "know how to use Word."

Word has hundreds of features, but a third of the time users employ only 5 commands[22]: Paste, Save, Copy, Undo and Bold. It takes several weeks of training to properly learn Word's advanced features; features that could help a publisher save many hundreds of hours of time. But most never do. I've been using Word since 1985, nearly forty years, and I've never taken a course. I don't even know what I don't know about how to extract the full power from the software.

I go on about this because it's a helpful way to get your head around why AI software is so very different from any software you've ever worked with. It doesn't come with a manual, not even a Quick Start guide. It comes with a blank screen and a question: "What can I help you with."

There's no menu bar, no button to push, no keyboard shortcuts. You ask a question, start a chat, and you get some answers. Let's see what Claude thinks about this.

Claude's response:

"There are several key differences between working with modern conversational AI like myself compared to traditional tools like Microsoft Word or Excel:

"1. Natural language interaction: With conversational AI, you can communicate your intent using everyday language rather than having to learn and navigate complex menus and functions. You simply explain what you want to accomplish conversationally.

"2. Contextual understanding: AI assistants maintain context and understand the flow of the conversation, allowing for more natural back-and-forth dialog. Traditional software has no contextual awareness from one command to the next.

"3. Adaptability: AI can dynamically adapt and respond to a wide variety of requests, while traditional tools are limited to a predefined set of functions. An AI assistant can help with writing, analysis, math, coding, ideation, and more within a single interface."

That was useful, but I wanted something easier to grasp. So I ask:

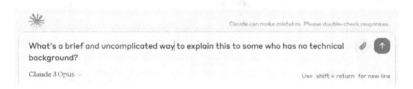

Claude:

"Here's a simple way to explain the difference to someone without a technical background:

"Think of traditional software like Microsoft Word or Excel as a tool, like a hammer or a calculator. It has a fixed set of functions that it can perform, and you need to learn how to use it properly to get the result you want.

"On the other hand, think of modern conversational AI as a smart assistant, like a knowledgeable colleague or friend. You can just talk to it using plain English, and it understands what you're trying to do. It can help you with all sorts of tasks, from writing to math to coming up with ideas.

"You don't need to learn any special commands or techniques—just chat with it naturally. It adapts to your needs and remembers the context of your conversation. Over time, it gets to know you and your preferences.

"So while traditional software is like a static tool that you use, conversational AI is more like an intelligent partner that you interact with naturally to get things done. It's a more flexible, personalized and efficient way of working."

Hmm. Not quite what I wanted. So I continued the conversation:

You're using terminology that non-technical people won't relate to, like "conversational AI" and "smart assistant." Try to explain it without those types of references.

Claude 3 Opus

Claude:

"Sure, let me try again without using technical terms:

"Imagine you're talking to a friend who is really knowledgeable and eager to help you out. You can just talk to them in plain English about what you're trying to do, whether it's writing an essay, solving a math problem, or brainstorming ideas for a project.

"Instead of having to learn and remember a bunch of specific steps or commands, you can just explain what you need in your own words. Your friend understands the context and adapts their help based on what you've already discussed.

"It's a back-and-forth conversation, where you can ask questions, clarify things, and get advice. And the more you talk to this friend, the better they understand your unique needs and communication style.

"Now, imagine if you could have that same type of helpful, easy interaction, but with a computer program. That's the basic idea behind new types of software you might be hearing about.

"Instead of the old style of software, where you have a rigid set of functions and have to learn the right way to use it, this new software is more like a knowledgeable friend. You can just talk to it conversationally and it figures out how to help you based on the natural flow of your discussion.

"So it's a smarter, more personalized, and easier way to get help with all sorts of tasks on your computer, just by talking to it like you would a person. That's the key difference from the older, more rigid style of software."

Summary: I was trying to do two things with these examples. One was to offer a dead simple instance of why chatbot software is so different from any software we've ever used. And the other was to illustrate how a chat can evolve. It's not just a single question and a single answer. It's a conversation. That's a big part of the breakthrough.

Chat AIs are 'school-trained', but inexperienced interns. You can't assume that they know what you mean. You need to explain what you want, why you want it, and how they can be most helpful. (I'll talk more about the related subject—prompting—below.)

Three kinds of AI software

 Using broad strokes, there are three kinds of AI software tools available today: foundational platforms, AI add-ons, and AI tools bolted onto existing products.

The first, AI foundational platforms, like ChatGPT, are core AI technology. The second, let's call them AI add-ons; software that's been freshly built on top of the core platforms. You won't have heard of many of these, tools like Jasper or Rewind.

My third category is software featuring AI tools perhaps crudely bolted onto their existing product. For example the Microsoft suite of software features new AI tools in Word, Excel and PowerPoint. Adobe has added AI technology to Photoshop and Acrobat. Grammarly is being rebuilt around the new generation of LLM-based technology. It's mostly the same product, but with AI added.

It's becoming clear that nearly all of the software you use today will soon enough incorporate AI features. You'll have to make your own assessment of whether those tools are genuinely useful or just AI window-dressing.

I'm more interested in the new tools, built from the ground up, to provide the value that only AI can engender. That's the next generation of software.

Working with AI Software

I'm a Windows guy, sadly (it's a long story as to why), and so I'm talking about my experiences accessing AI software via a Windows computer, not a Mac. Because all of the software here is browser-based, there shouldn't be a difference using these tools on a Mac. But I offer no guarantees.

You will need some money to play the AI game, but not a helluva lot. As described above, most of the foundational software can be accessed via free versions. You may want a paid subscription to get the full features, while you test it, and the subscription should be about $20/month. Cancel after you've tried it (don't forget!). If you see something that's $79/month or, god forbid, $159/month, you can ignore it. They're not thinking of you as a potential customer; they're thinking of large corporate users.

Training for Chat AI

 Today's AI is deceptively simple. Anyone who can type a question can use it. But using it well is complicated, which makes no apparent sense, until you dive into the complexities around "prompts" and related concepts.

In order to access its intelligence sometimes you have to talk to it as if it were an idiot. Or perhaps an idiot savant[23].

Anyone can use ChatGPT. Just go to chatgpt.com and you can access the most recent versions, GPT-4o, and o1, for free (there are some premium features available[24] for an extra $20/month).

When you go to ChatGPT you find essentially a blank screen and the question "How can I help you today?"

You can ask it questions. Better still, you can upload a large PDF and ask questions of the file. You can also upload images, which it can describe, or a scanned page: it can recognize the text, even if handwritten.

Prompts and prompting

Learning how to 'speak' with Chat AI has become an essential skill for everyone using today's Chat AI. You can literally speak to Chat AI in the latest mobile versions, but prompting is a special kind of language, and initially feels unnatural. Users discover that the more precise and detailed their prompts are, the better the responses they receive from ChatGPT. Further, prompts are not just one-off. Chat AI can continue a conversation for quite a while, and if you don't get the answer you're looking for you can revise and refine your prompts. This takes a lot of getting used to, and has spawned a series of how-tos, written and online, to train users on how to get the most out of prompting.

Try asking any of the Chat AI software to explain a concept like developmental editing. Then ask it to craft an explanation that a 12-year-old could understand. The results are dramatically different. Amusingly, Chat AI seems also to respond to emotional pleas. Adding "this is very important to my career" to a prompt can coax more useful responses.

(It's both reassuring and deeply troubling that the top scientists working on language-based AI are unable to explain why things like this occur.)

How to prompt

 "Prompting" is a specific skill that's essential to using Chat AI effectively.

Just now I asked ChatGPT to list "the top 4 elements of effective prompting":

1. Specific task instruction: Say exactly what you want the model to do.
2. Relevant context: Provide every fact, excerpt, or data point the model should rely on—don't make it guess.
3. Clear role/voice—Assign a persona or perspective ("You are an acquisitions editor...") to set the tone and expertise.
4. Output format & constraints: Tell the model how the answer should look (structure, length, citation style).

In a sense it's quite odd: AI has a good grasp of language—shouldn't it have a sense of what you mean without pedantic prompting? But it's precisely that mastery of language that makes prompting most powerful. Tell it exactly what you mean, not approximately—Chat AI understands complex instructions, in fact it thrives on them.

Talk to it like the helpful assistant, or the counselor, that you want it to be, not like a kid off the street.

The takeaway here is that, at least for the time being, the effective use of LLM-based AI tools requires conversancy with prompting best practices. A prompting *mastery* will be appropriately rewarded.

I'm going to include two links to prompting guides that can help you go a few steps deeper. *Beware*: The rules for prompting change as the software evolves, and a guide from 2023 is mostly by now misleading. These two were written or revised in April 2025:

1. Prompt Engineering (Montana State University Library)[25]
2. Prompt engineering guide: IBM[26]

Hallucinations:
A Fly in the Ointment

 AI, based in large language models, makes stuff up. It just does. This is generally called "hallucinations." It's a real problem, a serious problem. You need to understand hallucinations if you're going to work with AI.

Cambridge Dictionary's Word of the Year for 2023 was "Hallucinate," whose definition has been expanded to include "When an artificial intelligence... hallucinates, it produces false information." (Other additions to the 2023 dictionary include "prompt engineering," "large language model," and "GenAI.")

AI hallucinations, Cambridge notes, "sometimes appear nonsensical. But they can also seem entirely plausible—even while being factually inaccurate or ultimately illogical." This, sadly, is quite true, and as of May 2025 remains a significant limitation for using generative AI for mission-critical tasks. It's one of the several great oddities of AI, and it takes people a while to get their heads around it. Remember, generative AI is mostly a next word prediction engine, not a database of facts. Hence the need for HITLs, Humans-In-The-Loop, as we're now known, double-checking AI output. And again, it's remarkable that we can get such extraordinary value from a technology that can produce provably inaccurate output. So it goes.

Gary Marcus, an experienced and well-informed AI-critic, compares AI hallucinations to broken watches[27], which are right twice a day. "It's right some of the time," he says, "but you don't know which part of the time, and that greatly diminishes its value."

Ethan Mollick, a hit keynote speaker at our *Publishers Weekly* September 2023 conference[28], notes that people using AI expect 100% accuracy. Hallucinations, he says, are similar to "human rates of error" which we tolerate daily.

Andrej Karpathy, a noted computer scientist specializing in AI, who worked at Tesla and OpenAI, writes about hallucinations:

> "I always struggle a bit when I'm asked about the 'hallucination problem' in LLMs. Because, in some sense, hallucination is all LLMs do. They are dream machines.
>
> "We direct their dreams with prompts. The prompts start the dream, and based on the LLM's hazy recollection of its training documents, most of the time the result goes someplace useful.
>
> "It's only when the dreams go into deemed factually incorrect territory that we label it a 'hallucination.' It looks like a bug, but it's just the LLM doing what it always does."

It's not just the problem of making stuff up. Chat AI is flawed in other ways. For many queries, particularly from novices, the responses are mundane, off-target or simply unhelpful. Chat AI often has trouble counting:

Ask it for a 500-word blog post and you might only get 150.

And each of the AI companies, in order to reduce bias and to avoid answering "how-to-build-a-bomb" queries, has erected tight response guardrails around their products: all too often, the response to a question is, essentially, "No, I won't answer that." I asked Google Gemini to review a draft of this text and was cautioned that "it's essential to get the author's approval before publishing."

It's getting (a lot) better

 Hallucinations are a technology problem, which will find a technology solution. Things are getting better already.

Consider this: When I was writing this book in the spring and early summer of last year (2024) I asked four Chat AI's to fact-check the following statements:

- As of 2024, there are 6 big multinational publishers based in New York City. They are known as the Big 6.
- Ebooks continue to dominate book sales in the United States.
- Borders and Barnes & Noble are the two largest bookselling chains in the United States.
- After a sales decline during Covid, U.S. book sales are again growing by double-digits.

All of them spotted the errors in the first three statements. Each of them became confused by the fourth, uncertain of the extent of the Covid sales bump, and of subsequent sales patterns.

Just now (April 2025) I tried the same questions, and ChatGPT and the others easily spotted the fallacy in #4.

So I made the questions a little tougher:

- As of 2025, there are 5 big American publishers based in New York City. What is the next tier of book publishers and how many are there?
- Ebooks continue to dominate digital book sales in the United States.
- Barnes & Noble sells more books than all of the independent bricks & mortar book sellers in the United States.
- U.S. book sales, adjusted for inflation, have grown significantly during the past 20 years.

Claude was the weakest in its responses, stumbling and tongue-tied. It didn't spot the latest data on audiobooks sales that shows them surpassing ebooks in several instances.

ChatGPT's latest model, o3, was better, but still superficial in the sources it consulted. So I moved onto its recent "Deep Research" mode with the same questions. It asked me a few clarifying questions and then began its research journey, apprising me of the specifics of its inquiries as it rattled along. At one point it noted "Taking a closer look at HarperCollins and Hachette's acquisitions, understanding the dynamics of pre- and post-acquisition publishers, and considering Amazon's imprints' emergence" and a little later "It's interesting to see the wide range of revenue estimates from various sources, indicating a need for further verification and comparison."

After 17 minutes it reported that it had completed its research after consulting 39 sources, and generated a 3500-word report. I asked for a downloadable version and it prepared an attractive 500-word summary with key conclusions and two tables.

Meanwhile Google's Gemini's 2.5 Pro model, after asking me to approve its research plan, proceeded, in three minutes, to generate a 3800-word report with two tables and 64 citations. I exported this to a well-formatted Google doc.

Both ChatGPT and Gemini struggled on some of the facts. I forgive them—I know from my own work how damnably difficult it is to get solid data on the U.S. publishing industry. Neither could identify more than a handful of second-tier publishers in the U.S. beyond the obvious candidates like Scholastic and W.W. Norton.

ChatGPT (based on a few ill-researched blog posts) calculated that Barnes & Noble sells 8% of print units in the U.S., while independents sell 5-6%. Gemini stated, more soberly, that "The statement 'Barnes & Noble sells more books than all of the independent bricks & mortar book sellers in the United States' is PLAUSIBLE but UNVERIFIABLE with current data."

Both understood that audiobook sales are starting to edge above ebooks, quoting figures from the AAP.

ChatGPT suggested that "real spending (on books) is roughly 25% lower (in 2023) than in 2005," while Gemini, with much detail, notes "a real decline of roughly 27% over 19 years" (to 2024).

Bottom line: ChatGPT Deep Research is, at a glance, impressive, but it shows no discernment in its sources and produces a report that doesn't stand up to scrutiny. Google Gemini, by comparison, is dazzling. I could have done a marginally better job, but it would have taken me three days, not three minutes.

ChatGPT Deep Research appeared only in February 2025; Gemini in late March. We're entering the next major AI era, and few publishers have yet heard about it.

What About Images and Video?

 Because trade book publishing is dependent more on text than on images, publishers tend to overlook the ground-breaking AI-based tools for images and video.

Images and Video are essential to anyone's understanding of the AI revolution. But the discussion is too large for the space available: I just wouldn't do it justice.

Recommended for authors and publishers: play with the image generation features in ChatGPT and Microsoft Copilot—they're free and fun to use. Then do a search under "video and AI" and marvel at some of the examples you'll find in the sites linked.

OpenAI's Sora's[29] site includes some stunning examples of videos generated just from text prompts, as does Google's Veo 2[30].

I've created a page on my blog[31] with some of my favorites.

Software for Book Publishers

There is very little built-from-the-ground-up AI software *specifically* for book publishers (though there's lots available for authors).

Scholarly publishers have many more options, with a variety of AI tools for research, writing and publishing.

For trade publishers most of the options relate to AI and audio. Outside of audio, the choices are coalescing around editing and marketing tools. There are also several AI content-detection tools, and content licensing tools and services.

The editing software is positioned towards authors, not professional editors—there are many more authors than editors.

The marketing tools likewise aim more broadly than just book publishers, but for marketers everywhere, with tools for web content, copy generation and SEO. Jasper.ai is a leader in this category, and claims HarperCollins as a customer.

Shimmr, a sponsor of this book, is an AI-powered ad creation tool specifically for book publishers. The company, and its founder, Nadim Sadek, were profiled in a May 2024 article in *Publishers Weekly*[32].

"What we do is use AI to consider the psychological profile of a book and match it to the frame of mind of a specific audience, ensuring a more effective connection between readers and books," Sadek told PW. "We call it 'Book DNA,' and it involves not only knowing the characters and plot of a book, but the values, interests, and emotions of the book."

Calling on the Book DNA, Shimmr's AI tools then create targeted advertisements for search and social media channels (currently Google and Meta). The ads take the form of display ads, featuring AI-generated images accompanied by taglines. (Shimmr tell me that video ads are in the works, as well as new advertising channels.)

I point out to publishers evaluating Shimmr that the software can generate incremental revenue, which is what we hope a new advertising/marketing tool can bring to the table.

Another new vendor born out of the opportunity with AI, is Veristage (also a sponsor of this book). Veristage offers Insight, its "AI Publishing Assistant," a task-specific front-end across multiple publishing functions.

The Insight journey starts with the manuscript. Uploading an early version unlocks a range of tools, some more valuable to editorial, others more valuable to marketing. After working with any and all of the features, you can download a PDF report that includes editorial aspects, like writing tone, tropes, cliches and use of adverbs and adjectives, and then marketing content, like descriptions, metadata, unique selling points, comps, Amazon-optimized content, and suggested social media posts.

What I like best about Insight is that it takes a holistic approach to applying AI to the publishing process, rather than having to gather multiple software tools, each for a different function.

I want also to highlight here Leanpub, the publishing platform that hosts this book. They've been amazing to work with. Small is beautiful: they take chances with technology and services that larger companies would steer away from. Of top interest to authors and smaller publishers is their new TranslateWord service[33], where you can translate a book written in Microsoft Word into up to 31 languages, via the GPT-4o API (which powers ChatGPT). That's what I'm using to translate this book.

I looked elsewhere to try to find an AI service for book translation. There are tons of translation firms, some employing AI. The only one I could find that offers book translation is DeepL[34]. But books and book publishing are not a focus for the company. Right now Leanpub is the place to go[35].

Business software for book publishing

 The existing business systems vendors serving the publishing industry are starting to layer in AI technologies, as we've seen at other enterprise-scale companies, like Salesforce[36] and Oracle[37].

I've spoken with several of the publishing system software vendors. They're all looking at the opportunities, but treading carefully.

knk has run two webinars on AI, and released a whitepaper[38], but, as of May 2025, had not announced any AI features in its products.

Virtusales has launched[39] its first set of AI-enabled tools, including image tagging, alt-text generation, copyediting tools, sales and marketing copy generation, and translations of that copy.

I spoke with Klopotek on its Klopotek Publishing Radio[40]. They have "started an AI initiative in the area of Customer Services[41]," and vaguely reference[42] partnering "with a specialist AI company to develop an integrated solution for modern publishers.

Supadu[43], which offers publishers "web design, ecommerce and data solutions," now features "Supadu Smart AI," (pdf[44] with "'avatar-led' video book reviews, fully integrated with Supadu Smart Buy Buttons, and easy author video translations for global markets."

AI software for book publishers: the startups

Some people are familiar with the work I've done around book publishing technology-based startups. There is a report in Publishers Weekly that describes the project[45], and also links to the database.

As you'll see in the report, I look pretty broadly at startups across the book publishing spectrum. I don't include new book publishing companies, unless they are doing some unusual things with technology. The basic criteria is: do you use technology to try to invigorate some aspect of the book(ish) publishing process? I've got over 1,800 companies in the database, most launched after Amazon released the first Kindle in 2007.

After you get an overall sense of the database, you can start to dive in more deeply. On the far right tab you'll see a way to sort only by the AI-related publishing startups.

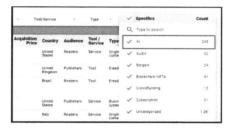

As you can see in the illustration, there are over 300 AI-related publishing startups (as of May 2025). We count the audio publishing startups that employ AI as a separate category and the total of the two is some 350 companies. The majority, over 280, were launched after ChatGPT first appeared in November of 2022. This volume of new business startups is unprecedented within book publishing. It's astounding.

As is characteristic of the full database, these AI startups mostly target authors (70%). Some 13% are looking, per se, to serve publishing companies. 10% are children's publishing-focused.

About 50 of the startups target readers with a range of inventive offerings. Several are storytelling platforms. There are quite a few summarizers. There are multiple discovery sites, "use AI to find your new favorite book."

Fast-improving AI-generated voices have led to a selection of "read it to me" tools.

As is characteristic of the larger startup cohort, many of these startups are between miniscule and tiny, just one person with a website and a half-baked idea. I include them all—who knows where they're headed.

I encourage you to play with the database. Click a few links. I think you'll be tickled by the innovation and audacity of many of these organizations.

One of the sponsors of this book, Book Advisors, specializes in mergers and acquisitions in the publishing industry. I'm always advocating to innovative startups that they look for partners, and Book Advisors is where I send them to talk through the process. Book publishing is served by several respected M&A firms, including The Fisher Company and Oaklins DeSilva+Phillips. Book Advisors is the only firm I know that also works with technology startups.

AI and Book Publishing: the Industry Associations

 The AI-related activities of many of the prominent publishing trade groups appear mainly to be adding their voices to the chorus of the copyright-concerned.

The Association of American Publishers[46] "filed reply comments in the U.S. Copyright Office inquiry into the intersection of copyright law and artificial intelligence (AI)..." The U.K. Publishers Association notes that[47] "it is of the utmost importance that the Government puts in place tangible solutions as soon as possible to protect the human creativity and knowledge that underpins safe and reliable AI."

On the other hand, the Independent Publishers Guild (IPG), with more than 600 members, offers AI guidance[48] and training to its members, including its "Practical Guide to AI in Publishing[49]," conducted by a noted AI and publishing expert, George Walkley[50].

Here in the U.S., I was privileged to be part of the Book Industry Study Group's (BISG) AI Working Group[51], which reports to the Workflow Committee[52]. The Working Group has outlined several potential strategic initiatives:

- Best Practices and Standards Development: Recommending best practices related to AI usage, linked to ethical guidelines, existing regulations, and laws. This includes transparency in AI-generated content and its disclosure to consumers.

- Industry Surveys and Definitions: Conducting surveys to gather broad industry insights on current and potential AI uses and establishing clear definitions and scopes for what AI means within the context of book publishing.
- Periodic Reporting and Reviews: Offering periodic reports to help the industry foresee and adapt to the rapid changes brought about by AI technologies.

Other writing and publishing associations are trying to get in front of the topic. Some take stands in opposition to AI; others are just trying to help their members understand the technology and, perhaps, to experiment with it.

What are Publishing Companies Doing About AI?

A year ago the question of what publishing companies are currently doing brought an answer of, "not much." Not a whole lot has changed since, but there has been some activity. I'll focus on trade book publishers; scholarly and academic publishers are more active. Here's some of what I've uncovered.

Hachette: According to a November 2023 report[53] in *The Bookseller* in the UK, Hachette has published a position statement on AI, offering a distinction between 'operational' uses and 'creative' uses. The company "made it clear it encourages 'responsible experimentation' for operational uses but is opposed to 'machine creativity... in order to protect original creative content produced by humans'."

HarperCollins: According to an April, 2023 report in *Publishers Weekly* by Andrew Albanese and Ed Nawotka, HarperCollins CEO Brian Murray said:

> "We know that it's going to be important and it's going to have a major impact on our industry over the next three to five years. And so I think a lot of us are trying to figure out how and to make sure we employ it in an ethical, moral way that helps us serve authors and provide professional services to authors

and doesn't compete with authors and story-telling.

"And that's, I think, a challenge. Not so much maybe for all the publishers that are here, but I guarantee you there are a lot of little tech teams around the world that might be coming after our business. They're not publishers, they're not editors. They're the technologists and they see an opportunity."

Penguin Random House (PRH): Bertelsmann, the parent company of PRH, offers a white paper[54] called *State of Play: Exploring Generative AI's Transformative Effects on the Media & Entertainment Industry*, which includes a section on book publishing.

Also, according to a report in *Publishers Lunch*[55], the company "introduced its own internal AI application, called PRH ChatGPT."

The article states that PRH internal documents explain that the program "'can be used to streamline processes, enhance creativity, and provide data insights' across departments. The company suggests that among the uses of the app are summarizing books and documents; revising emails; drafting blog posts or job descriptions; analyzing text-based data, and "generat[ing] ideas for content."'

Simon & Schuster: Company CEO Jonathan Karp earned a mention in the *New York Times* "Most Memorable Literary Moments of the Last 25 Years" with a quote reported in *Publishers Weekly* from its May 2024 U.S. Book Show[56]. He said that AI was not the "elephant in the room" but rather, "more like the cicada in the world. You know, lots of buzzing and lots of screwing."

He acknowledged that AI "is definitely a valuable tool. It's definitely going to make us more efficient. It's going to help us process and gather information better, and hopefully allow workers to do a higher level of work that's more interesting and creative."

In March 2024, at the London Book Fair, as reported in *The Bookseller*, Karp said that the company would also be looking at foreign language versions of AI-generated audiobooks "in territories where [that author's] works would never otherwise have a chance because of the cost of [audio production]."

AI and Book Publishing: The Use Cases

 The specific use cases for AI and book publishing, across different functions, are easy to describe conceptually. But there's not much information available about what publishers are actually doing.

Keith Riegert, CEO of Ulysses Press and Perfect Bound, presented at the *Publishers Weekly* U.S. Book Show in May 2024[57], offering the most comprehensive overview I've seen about AI use cases within publishing companies. Though Perfect Bound is a sponsor of this report, I stand by that statement. Keith offers "20 practical ways you, as a publishing professional, can start using AI right now."

His presentation, *Getting Started with AI*, can be viewed and downloaded from[58] the Perfect Bound website.

AI for book design & production

 Expert systems and process automation are still ahead of AI when it comes to book design and production.

Software for the automated typesetting of books dates back to at least the 1970s. In the mid-1980s I supervised a software project called PageOne, based on Donald Knuth's TeX[59], which could typeset a book in minutes. SGML appeared[60] around the same time, based on a document standard introduced in 1969. It was largely succeeded by XML, introduced in 1996. These robust markup languages create solid structures for automation.

Desktop publishing ushered in another round of automation for QuarkXPress and Adobe InDesign, as well as Adobe Illustrator and Adobe Photoshop. Publishing workflows can be managed with various programs and systems.

An organization to watch is the Coko Foundation[61]. They offer a suite of open source production and publishing management tools, including Kotahi, a scholarly publishing platform, and Ketty for book production, which includes an AI Assistant[62]. The Kotahi AI PDF Designer[63], "transforms PDF design into a straightforward, interactive process."

There are some early initiatives to bring AI into InDesign workflows. In April 2024 Adobe announced a Text to Image feature[64]. Third parties may be getting ahead of Adobe here: the innovative prepress and editorial production vendors in India, such as Hurix Digital[65] and Integra[66], are showing more initiative than Adobe in harnessing AI for production.

AI & book marketing

> AI's impact on book marketing will be shallow in the short term; more profound over time. A lot depends on what you perceive 'book marketing' to be; it's changing.

The 'low-hanging fruit' for AI in marketing seems obvious. Ask Chat AI to help with a product description or a press release. Ask it to suggest some keywords. This it can do, without breaking a sweat. But most publishing professionals can do the same thing, with only a little moisture on the brow.

Keith Riegert's use cases, linked above, include suggestions for brainstorming titles, drafting a digital marketing report, and creating a digital marketing campaign tracker in Google Sheets.

Shimmr software, described above, hints at the shape of automated marketing to come.

Veristage[67] (a sponsor of this book) supports marketing and sales activities, including helping you define the target audience for a book, and its unique selling points, and can provide auto-generated advertising copy to be used in marketing, email, PR, and social campaigns.

AI and metadata

> What does AI have to do with metadata, and vice versa? It's role appears modest thus far; expect some big changes.

Metadata is core to book discoverability. You've heard that enough times to be nauseated by the admonition. It's off-putting mainly because "metadata" remains elusive to most non-techies. If you say, "it's just the basic info about the book, the title, description, price, subject categories, that kind of thing," people exhale. That they're comfortable with. But that's about all.

I regret to remind you that there's actually far more to metadata than just a few details about the book. There's so much more. Much more than I can encompass in this little book. I've co-authored a whole book on the topic[68]. Ingram publishes *Metadata Essentials*, an excellent short volume[69]. I'll say it here, and not for the last time: authors and publishers pay short-shrift to their metadata at their peril.

AI can help with metadata generation. For example, self-publishing vendor PublishDrive, offers an "AI-Powered Book Metadata Generator"[70] which offers AI recommendations for the book title, blurb, Amazon categories, BISAC categories, and keywords.

Insight, from Veristage[71], described above, can generate descriptions, keywords, and define optimal BISAC categories.

Declaring AI use in metadata

 In November, 2023, EDItEUR, the keeper of the ONIX standard, released a short Application Note called "Aspects of AI in ONIX." (pdf[72])

With his typical deep wisdom, Graham Bell, EDItEUR's director, notes that "one reaction to (the controversies surrounding AI) is to forswear use of AI or to avoid trading in AI-created products. A more realistic option is simply to be transparent with trading partners and readers when AI has been used. And as some resellers limit or ban AI-based content from their platforms, it is important for reputable publishers to highlight those products that do use generative AI techniques to create content."

Bell goes on to outline ways that publishers can specify in metadata:

- AI contributors
- AI-based voices in audiobooks

... as well as a method to indicate in the metadata for digital products that the publisher explicitly opt outs of text and data mining (TDM) for uses other than research. There's also a way to specify a separate license covering commercial TDM.

As is often that case, what is specified in ONIX may not be uncovered down the food chain, but at least a best effort has been made.

AI Strategies for Book Publishing Companies

Here's a draft roadmap for implementing AI in a book publishing company.

1. AI Adoption Decision: Decision-makers need to understand the fundamentals of AI as it impacts publishing, and to be willing to make a series of decisions about AI within their organization. If you decide to move forward with AI, there's no point in moving tepidly. You'll learn little from gingerly poking AI around the edges — you'll get the impression that it offers little value. The only useful approach is to go all in.

2. Digital Readiness Audit: Before you move forward with specific AI initiatives, you need to get your "digital house" in order. Any existing workflow problems that your publishing company still faces should be addressed NOW, because the company needs to approach AI from a position of digital operational strength. Is your metadata complete, accurate and up to date? Are all of your backlist books digitized, with the content consistently tagged? Are you efficiently using a sufficiently robust TMS and/or CMS (title management system or content management system)?

3. Staffing for AI: See section below.

4. AI Training: See the section "Some Additional Sources" below for training resources beyond this book.

5. Pilot Project: Plan for a pilot project to be implemented by the early enthusiasts. Don't make it too easy, but make sure it's a win. Create a framework for evaluating the project; determine success metrics (e.g., improved efficiency, cost reduction, or enhanced user experience).

6. Financial Planning: You will need to budget for AI training and implementation. Software costs are modest; nearly all of the costs are in training and recruitment. Larger initiatives will require the skills of consultants and outside vendors. Where will the funding come from for your AI initiatives? Can you project a ROI? I've created a somewhat arbitrary goal for book publishing companies looking to adopt AI technologies: look to drive 15% out of your fixed costs while building the sales of backlist titles by 15%.

7. AI & Publishing Value Chain: Analyze how AI could disrupt various aspects of the publishing value chain, such as author discovery, editorial processes, book production, marketing, and distribution. How will these disruptions impact your organization? What actions do you need to take to minimize the effects of the disruption?

8. 1-2 Year AI Strategy: Create an internal task force to build out a 1-year and 2-year AI strategy for your organization. Anything past 2 years is wild speculation — arguably even with a 1-year and 2-year AI strategy. But in times of uncertainty, planning is an essential discipline. With each perceived opportunity, decide whether you are creating organizational efficiencies with AI (cost savings), or driving new revenue. Regardless of the anticipated dollars that might be saved, or the revenue that might be gained, assume that both types of initia-

tives have equal value. Nonetheless, set targets and timelines. Given the speed of change for AI, include quarterly review/adjustment cycles.

9. AI Quality Control: Establish metrics for evaluating AI output quality across different departments. Define acceptable error rates and correction procedures. Create workflows for human review and oversight.

10. Industry Allies: Figure out who your allies are, whether at other publishing companies or at trade associations, or just enthusiastic individuals/analysts/consultants. Reach out and confer. Hire outside talent to analyze, to advise, and to assist. Attend industry conferences and online webinars.

11. Vendor Assessment: Make a first assessment on which vendors or other service partners might be able to provide software or systems-based approaches to move the organization forward with AI technology.

12. Competitor AI Analysis: Assess what your competitors are doing with AI. What outcomes do you expect them to achieve from their efforts? How should this impact your strategy?

13. AI Policy Development: See next section for more.

14. Data security and privacy: Implement safeguards for the use of AI tools for manuscripts and associated data. Ensure GDPR and CCPA compliance when using AI. Evaluate other regulations within the U.S. federal and state governments.

15. AI Risk Management: Create contingency plans for AI program failures. Develop protocols for AI-related PR issues. Plan for potential AI regulatory changes.

16. Author Relations: Create support systems for authors using AI tools. Develop AI collaboration

guidelines. Plan a communication strategy around AI initiatives. Consider programs to educate your authors on the pluses and minuses of engaging with AI.

17. AI Use Detection, Fact-checking and Plagiarism Detection: Invest in understanding which AI tools can detect AI use, plagiarism or inappropriate content. Explore AI use for fact-checking.

18. Accessibility and AI: AI tools are proving to be fast and largely accurate for creating accessible content, including both alt-text and audiobooks. How can you take advantage of these tools?

19. AI for Marketing: AI tools for marketing have tremendous potential and are being widely used across multiple industries. Your staff need to prioritize AI adoption across marketing and sales functions.

20. AI & Audiobooks: The technology for synthetic voices works today, and is essentially undetectable. Determine your strategy on the use of AI for audiobooks, particularly for backlist.

21. AI & Translation: AI translations using large language models greatly increase translation efficiency. What does this mean to your strategy of selling and buying foreign-language rights? Which of your books could you translate to Spanish, just for the U.S. market?

22. The Long-Term Vision: While acknowledging the limitations of long-term predictions, brainstorm some visionary thinking about the future of AI in publishing, including potential scenarios and their implications for the industry. Encourage an internal team of enthusiasts to explore speculative AI innovations, including AGI (artificial general intelligence).

Developing and communicating
AI policies

Despite its widespread use, few publishers have publicly defined their AI policies, and communicated their approach to AI to the public. The term 'the public' has a slippery significance here, when you consider the different publics addressed by trade, scholarly and educational publishers.

For trade publishers the most important audience is authors and their agents. Scholarly publishers face different obstacles, when they consider AI's promising impact on research, and then AI's more problematic impact upon converting research into narrative (Avi Staiman wrote a thoughtful post on this topic[73]). For educational publishers, establishing policies is tricky, as AI's encroachment on the practice of teaching, of education, is multifaceted and complex.

Publishers face two big challenges as they move forward with AI technologies. The first is to develop a corporate position about how to approach AI generally, on how to incorporate AI into their workflows. The second challenge is communicating their position, clearly and unambiguously, to their constituents.

The publisher policies I have seen are mostly flawed. Some of them are in fact policies directed externally, *at* authors, with a range of admonitions about what is acceptable practice (not much) and what is not acceptable (lots). O'Reilly's "AI Use Policy for Talent Developing Content for O'Reilly"[74] goes on for pages and pages, with esoteric guidance, such as "DO NOT use any OSS GenAI Models that produce software Output that is subject to the terms of a copyleft or network viral open source license."

On the other hand scholarly publisher Elsevier, in the "Elsevier Policies"[75] section of its website, includes statements on "Responsible AI Principles," "Text and Data Mining," and "The use of generative AI and AI-assisted technologies in writing for Elsevier."

The few internal, unpublished, publisher policies that I've seen are conservative, excessively so. These publishers reacted too quickly to the range of perceived and possible threats, and to their authors' anxieties, and have hamstrung their own ability to engage robustly with this fast-developing, fast-changing technology.

It's a given that they will use AI 'responsibly,' whatever that means. It's a given that they have the utmost concern for authors' intellectual property and for aggressively protecting author's copyrighted work. (Although, of course, these principles must be declared publicly, and often reiterated.)

But what else?

- Will they allow AI to have *a role* in editorial acquisitions? Can AI take a look at the slush pile?
- Will they allow AI to have *a role* in developmental editing, line editing and copyediting?
- Will they allow AI to have *a role* in determining print runs and allocations?
- In creating accessible ebook files, including alt-text?
- In aiding audiobook creation in cases where it's not economically-realistic to hire talented human narrators?

- In aiding foreign language translation into markets where rights would never be sold?
- In developing marketing material at scale?
- In communicating with resellers?

If so they must make this clear, and clearly explain, the thinking behind these policies. Publishers must be brave in countering the many objections of most authors at this time of fear and doubt.

Job considerations

 Only the largest publishers will be able to hire dedicated staff to work with AI software and systems. The average publisher will want to expose all of their staff to AI tools, expecting that each might explore using AI to find efficiencies in their work.

Management can't tackle AI on their own, and they can't tackle it just with outside vendors and consultants. Your success in executing your overall AI strategy will be determined by whether you can get buy-in from your knowledgeable and experienced publishing team.

Some of your staff have already made progress on their own, probably without your support or explicit endorsement. Try to identify the enthusiasts on your staff. ...strategic direction?

At the February 2024 PubWest conference in Arizona a speaker from outside the publishing industry suggested that one of the uses for AI will be replacing interns. The room burst into flames. She meant well—indeed an April 10, 2024 report in the *New York Times*[76] describes how Wall Street investment banks are looking to replace many of their interns with AI. Similar to the case in publishing, an obvious concern is: how do you find senior analysts if they can't start off as junior analysts?

The publishing industry has always relied on internships. A 2019 study[77] found that 80 percent of the people who had worked in publishing for less than fifteen years had previously interned.

In part it's a way to get the grunt work dispatched at a reasonable cost. But that pales against the larger reality that no publishing school can equip someone to join a publishing company at the level of middle-manager. The only way to develop the skilled staff of tomorrow is to train interns and apprentices today.

The objective here is not to seek to replace interns with AI, but instead to make their work more productive and rewarding using AI tools, benefitting both the intern and the publishing company.

AI for Audiobooks

 AI for audiobooks works really well. It's not perfect, but it works. Authors and publishers are now routinely using AI tools in audiobook production, primarily for books where full-scale narrator-focused audiobook production is not financially feasible. And not only for English-language audiobooks, but also audiobooks in translation.

Using AI for audiobooks is not new; I first reported on the trend in *Publishers Weekly* in 2021[78]. But the latest AI technology has reinvigorated the opportunity for automated audiobook narration.

Back in 2021 I noted "Is it perfect? Certainly not. Can it be good enough? Probably, if a publisher is willing to spend the necessary time in the voice editing phase of the project." Four years later, by many accounts, AI-voices are undetectable from human voices, unless you're listening very closely.

Last November Meta (Facebook) introduced "Seamless[79]," which is able to "transfer tones, emotional expression, and vocal style qualities" into the translation of 200 languages. An audiobook can be immediately translated into multiple languages with extraordinary quality.

Also in 2021 I reported that "Audible's block on the distribution of audiobooks with non-human narrators is a real problem that may take some time to resolve."

In the meantime, both Google and Apple announced programs to allow authors to create audiobooks with AI-generated voices. On December 5, 2023, Findaway Voices by Spotify began accepting "digital voice narrated audiobooks from Google Play Books for distribution to select retail partners."

In early November 2023 Amazon announced that Kindle Direct Publishing (KDP) authors would soon have access to a service, "Virtual Voice," that would allow them to "quickly and easily produce an audiobook version of their ebook using virtual voice narration, a synthetic speech technology." In January 2024, Jane Friedman reported (paywall[80]) "Audible quietly started allowing AI-narrated audiobooks to enter its storefront late last fall, long after other retailers had done the same."

Then, on May 13, 2025, Audible announced that it would be "bringing new audiobooks to life through our own fully integrated, end-to-end AI production technology." *Publishers Weekly*, covering the announcement[81], suggested that Audible's competitors, like Spotify and Storytel, had forced the action.

Alongside the audio AI announcement was a nod to AI translation, that it will "begin rolling out... in beta later in 2025, allowing select publishers to bring their audiobooks to international audiences in their local languages. We're developing support for translations from English to Spanish, French, Italian and German, which we'll begin to roll out throughout this year."

These endorsements change the playing field. They are creating opportunities for authors and their licensees to earn more money. That's impossible to ignore.

AI for Book Translation

 AI for book translation works. Non-literary fiction could be first. Literary fiction may follow. Nonfiction poses a different set of challenges.

I hosted a webinar on AI for book translation, sponsored by BISG, in June 2024. The video is online on YouTube[82].

The subject is complex and nuanced. One thing I find fascinating is how long people have been trying to automate translation. It's a reminder that books, which fill our universe, are such a small proportion of written communication, even more so in this online age.

Warren Weaver, credited as the father of machine translation (MT), noted to a colleague, "When I look at an article in Russian, I say: 'This is really written in English, but it has been coded in some strange symbols. I will now proceed to decode.'" For a machine, language is just a code. It's not culture and feeling and the grandeur of written language. It's a task where letters can be converted to numbers.

Clearly the fiction/nonfiction divide will loom large in AI translation. Chat AI is strong on style, but it can fall short on facts. Literary fiction is the elephant in the room. It is precious and revered and rightly so. Translators can spend hours arguing about a single word or phrase. Chat AI must tread cautiously in those waters.

But this is fertile territory. As far as I can determine (from scant data), there were only 9,500 trade book translations into English in 2023. Even if I'm off by a large factor, it's clear that few books are being translated from foreign languages into English.

Similarly, I found a statistic indicating that in 2023 there were only 7,230 translations from English into Spanish (in Spanish book markets). That seems ludicrously small. (And, according to a colleague in Spain, is a significant underestimate. But still...)

There's a vast opportunity here.

Most of the use of AI for book translation will be for books where translation was never considered economically feasible. There is bound to be a job impact on translators of "mid-market" books; the job growth will be managing projects and in QA. Will that offset the job loss? Unlikely.

As with most aspects of AI, there are complex challenges to be addressed, and no easy answers.

As noted above, Leanpub and DeepL are two companies offering AI-assisted book translation services. Audible's May 2025 announcement, referenced above, brings translation also to audiobooks.

AI for Scholarly Publishing

 Trade publishers and authors of all stripes would do well to keep an eye on AI's trajectory in the scholarly publishing community. It's advancing far more rapidly than in consumer publishing.

I see a couple of reasons for the advance within this community. First, the authors within scholarly publishing are academics by trade, and in the STEM sector (science, technology, engineering, and mathematics), they're often scientists with advanced degrees. Quite apart from publishing, they are investigating, and often embracing, AI within their research work. They would be more surprised to find that their publisher was *not* exploring the use of AI in editing and publishing their work.

This flows up into the scholarly publishing ecosystem, where, as often as not, the editors are scholars themselves. For them, technology is not intimidating; it part of their everyday work.

I'm not going to drill down further on the particulars in this book; I'll report on it in more depth on my blog.

AI for Authors

Authors and publishers seem sometimes to be living in two solitudes, connected, but apart.

Times change. Where publishers were once masters of the universe, top authors now call the shots. As I discuss elsewhere, self-published authors are the trailblazers. They carry little of the cultural baggage that burdens traditional publishing.

When publishers look at AI, they see few opportunities. When I talk to authors about AI, the world is their oyster. The possibilities are near-endless:

Authoring and editing

- Trying to write & publish whole books
- Trying to ideate for a new project
- Trying to ideate within a new book
- Fine-tuning of the story
- Research
- Fact-checking
- Writing companion
- Developmental editing
- Copyediting
- Spell-checking and grammar-checking
- Proofreading

Illustration/imaging

- Create illustrations and charts
- Cover design roughs
- Video promotions

Marketing

- Automate submissions to agents, publishers, contests, friends, blurb requests
- Generate marketing material: press releases, blog posts, social media, etc.
- Website generation

Authors are going to drive much of the change in industry adoption of AI, whether for or against.

They are the beneficiaries of much of the startup innovation surrounding AI in authoring and publishing — some 70% of the startups are looking to work with authors on their journeys.

Sudowrite[83] is the leading software for fiction authors. Future Fiction Academy[84] offers both software and training.

Concerns and Risks Surrounding AI

 The concerns around AI are serious. The risks are real. Sometimes they are expressed in hysterical ways, but, when you drill down, the impact of AI has the potential to be enormously destructive.

The many issues and concerns surrounding AI can fill volumes on their own. Here's a word cloud of the topics I monitor. I'm sure I'm missing a few.

There's lots of information available on each of these topics, and I encourage you to read as deeply as you can. It's possible you'll conclude that the risks outweigh the benefits, and that you don't want to pursue the use of AI, whether personally or within your organization. In the end it's a personal choice.

If you google "books regarding the risks of AI" you'll find a selection of worthwhile volumes. A recent podcast that I found particularly chilling was Ezra Klein's chat with Dario Amodei[85], Anthropic's co-founder and CEO (the company that develops Claude.ai). You learn that these companies are aware of the risks. Amodei refers to an internal risk classification system called A.S.L., for "AI Safety Levels" (not American Sign Language). We're currently at ASL 2[86], "systems that show early signs of dangerous capabilities—for example ability to give instructions on how to build bioweapons." He describes ASL 4 as "enabling state-level actors to greatly increase their capability... where we would worry that North Korea or China or Russia could greatly enhance their offensive capabilities in various military areas with AI in a way that would give them a substantial advantage at the geopolitical level." Chilling stuff.

Within this grim context, I'll highlight the most pertinent issues for writers and publishers.

Copyright infringed?

 The copyright issues are a miasma of complexity and ambiguity. It appears certain that some books still in copyright were included in the training of some LLMs. But it's certainly not the case, as many authors fear, that all of their work was hoovered up into the large language models.

The copyright issues are both specific and broad. It's well-known that many of the LLMs were trained on the open web—everything that can be scraped from the 1.5 billion sites on the web today, whether it's newspaper articles, social media posts, Wikipedia, web blogs and, apparently, transcripts of YouTube videos.

It's provable[87] that at least one of the LLMs ingested the actual text of thousands of books not in the public domain. Possibly[88] others did as well.

Was it legal to ingest all of this text to help build billion-dollar AI companies, without any compensation to the authors? The AI companies make their argument around fair use; the courts will eventually decide. Even if it was legal, was it ethical or moral? The ethics appear less complex than the legal considerations. You decide.

The laws surrounding copyright obviously did not anticipate the unique challenges that AI brings to the issue, and searching for legal solutions will take time, probably years.

Here's a catalog of fifteen of the most prominent suits[89], not all of them having to do with books, but also images and music. And here's another list[90] that updates the status of all of the, by their count, 30 lawsuits.

Copyright and AI for authors

 Authors face additional issues surrounding the copyright-ability of AI-generated content.

The U.S. Copyright Office's position on[91] the copyright-ability of AI-generated content states that AI alone cannot hold copyright because it lacks the legal status of an author. That makes sense. But this assumes 100% of the work is AI-generated. As discussed elsewhere, few authors are going to let AI generate an entire book. More likely it will be 5%, or 10% or... And here the Copyright Office stumbles (as would I).

In a more recent ruling the Office concluded that a graphic novel comprised of human-authored text combined with images generated by the AI service Midjourney constituted a copyrightable work, but that the individual images themselves could not be protected by copyright." Jeez!

At the end of July the Office published[92] "Part 1 of its report on the legal and policy issues related to copyright and artificial intelligence, addressing the topic of digital replicas."

The New York Times offers a glimpse[93] into how the Copyright Office "is reviewing how centuries-old laws should apply to artificial intelligence technology, with both content creators and tech giants arguing their cases."

 Suffice it to say that authors and publishers need to be alert to evolving copyright challenges, on multiple fronts.

What are the long-term implications?

Some compare the current litigation to the Google books lawsuit[94], which took 10 years to legally resolve. Who knows how long the appeals process will drag out for these filings.

But that may not be a publisher's most serious issue. It's perception. AI is radioactive within the writing and publishing community. For many authors the well has been poisoned. Anything that even smacks of AI draws intense criticism.

There are numerous examples. In a recent incident Angry Robot, a UK publisher "dedicated to the best in modern adult science fiction, fantasy and WTF," announced that it would be using AI software, called Storywise[95], to sort through an anticipated large batch of manuscript submissions. It took just five hours[96] for the company to drop the plan and return to the "old inbox.[97]"

The startup Prosecraft[98], "the world's first (and only!) linguistic database of literary prose" was shut down in the blink of an eye[99].

The unbearable dilemma for trade publishers in using AI tools internally: if your authors find out, you'll have a hard time weathering the resulting storm. I believe that publishers have no choice but to be brave, to adopt (at least some of) the tools, explain clearly how those tools are trained and how they're utilized, and push on.

In the UK, The Society of Authors takes a hardline approach[100]: "Ask your publisher to confirm that it will not make substantial use of AI for any purpose in connection with your work—such as proof-reading, editing (including authenticity reads and fact-checking), indexing, legal vetting, design and layout, or anything else without your consent. You may wish to forbid audiobook narration, translation, and cover design rendered by AI."

The Authors Guild appears to accept that "publishers are starting to explore using AI as a tool in the usual course of their operations, including editorial and marketing uses." I don't think that many members of the Guild are as understanding.

Licensing content to AI companies

Many publishers, and not-as-many authors, are searching for ways to license content to AI companies. Everyone has a different idea of what the licensing terms should be, and how much their content is worth, but at least the discussions are underway. There's a general sense across the industry that agreeing to licensing deals now lessens the argument that the AI vendors had no choice but to seize copyrighted works. At the same time there's a sense of "well, they stole all of our books anyway. We might as well earn something from the theft."

Various LLM vendors have taken licenses for specific content, some books, but mostly news, social media, and other online text and data. Are the AI companies only going to license the *crème de la crème* of content? Do they need the skim milk as well? Are their relatively few licenses just window-dressing to mitigate damages if they lose the big lawsuits?

There are also concerns about discoverability. If your published work cannot be—in some manner—referenced via AI searches and conversations, does it become less visible? I'll talk more about AI and search below.

In early 2025 the publishing industry was startled to learn that HarperCollins had struck a deal with one of the large LLM companies for a 3-year license for an unspecified number of nonfiction backlist titles. The deal itself wasn't startling, but the terms were—$5,000/title, to be split 50/50 with the book author(s). No one I've spoken with expected books to command more than perhaps $100 per title, and as of May 2025, no other deals of a similar size have emerged.

There are several startups looking to work with publishers (and, in one case, individual authors). ProRata.ai[101] and Created by Humans[102] are both interesting in this regard.

In mid-July 2024, Copyright Clearance Center (CCC), long the publishing industry's top player for collective copyright licensing, announced[103] the availability of "artificial intelligence (AI) re-use rights within its Annual Copyright Licenses (ACL), an enterprise-wide content licensing solution offering rights from millions of works to businesses that subscribe." This is not a blanket license.

Publishers Weekly covered the announcement[104], quoting Tracey Armstrong, president and CEO of CCC, as saying "It is possible to be pro-AI and pro-copyright, and to couple AI with respect for creators."

It's not all-encompassing, covering only[105] "internal, not public, use of the copyrighted materials." Nonetheless, this could be a milestone in moving publishing closer to a degree of cooperation with the large language model developers.

It's too late to avoid AI

 For authors and publishers who prefer not to be sullied with AI, the news is bad: you're using AI today, and have been using it for years.

In the next few sections I want to dance around the ambiguities surrounding AI use. I'll try to walk you through the issues, many of them interrelated.

Artificial intelligence, in different forms, has already been integrated into most of the software tools and services we use every day. People rely on AI-powered spell- and grammar-checking in programs like Microsoft Word and Google Docs. Microsoft Word and PowerPoint apply AI to provide writing suggestions, to offer design and layout recommendations, and more. Virtual assistants like Siri and Alexa use natural language processing to understand voice commands and respond to questions. Email services leverage AI to filter messages, detect spam, and send alerts. AI powers customer service chatbots and generates product recommendations based on your purchase history and queries.

And much of this is based on Large Language Models, as it is with Chat AI.

For an author or editor to say, "I don't want AI used on my manuscript," is, broadly speaking, all but impossible, unless both they and their editors work with typewriters and pencils.

They could try saying, "I don't want generative AI" used on their book. But that's a tough one to slice and dice. Grammar-checking software was not originally built on generative AI. Grammarly has added AI[106] as an ingredient to its product, as will all other spelling and grammar checkers. Generative AI is also core to the marketing software on offer.

When authors use AI

Another aspect of authors and the use of AI has similarities to the copyright issue discussed above. In the extreme, we're seeing 100% AI-generated content being published on Amazon. Most of it (all of it?) is of terrible quality, but that doesn't prevent it from being published. (See also the Amazon section.) More concerning for publishers is AI-generated submissions. Yes, AI ups the quantity, but large publishers already have a filter for quantity. The filters are called agents. They are the ones who are going to have to figure out how to handle the quantity problem, and apparently they're going to have to find a solution that doesn't employ AI.

It's something of an existential problem—do I want to publish a book written by 'a machine'? For most publishers that's an unequivocal 'no.' Easy peasy. Well, what about a book where 50% of the content was generated by an LLM, under a capable author's supervision?

Hmm, let's try a 'no' on that as well. OK: then what about 25%, or 10%, or 5%? Where do you draw the line?

And, now that you've entered the line-drawing business, how do you resolve the dilemma that spelling and grammar tools now rely, at least in part, on generative AI[107]? What about AI-driven transcription tools, like Otter.ai[108], or the transcription feature built into Microsoft Word[109]?

I can't find any trade publisher that has declared they will not publish a work with a pre-specified quantity of AI-generated text. Here's the Authors Guild on the topic[110]:

> "If an appreciable amount of AI-generated text, characters, or plot are incorporated in your manuscript, you must disclose it to your publisher and should also disclose it to the reader. We don't think it is necessary for authors to disclose generative AI use when it is employed merely as a tool for brainstorming, idea generation, or for copyediting."

Needless to say, 'appreciable' is not defined (Oxford defines it as "large enough to be noticed or thought important"), but the post goes on to explain that the inclusion of more than *"de minimis* AI-generated text"* would violate most publishing contracts. *De minimis*, in legal terms, is not precisely specified, but, generally speaking, means more or less the same as appreciable.

Can AI be reliably detected in writing?

I hosted a webinar on AI detection, sponsored by BISG, in May 2024. The replay is online on YouTube[111]. Jane Friedman offered a comprehensive write-up of the webinar[112] in her *Hot Sheet* newsletter.

For many authors, the toxicity of AI means keeping it far away from their words. Publishers bear a special burden—they don't create the text, but, once published, they shoulder a substantial obligation to the text. We've seen lots of dynamite blow near incendiary books, whether it be around the social implications of the content, or the plagiaristic purloining of other writer's words and ideas. Now with AI we face a whole new set of ethical and legal issues, none of which were outlined in publishing school.

Part of it seems similar to what people worry about for students, that using AI is somehow cheating, similar to cribbing from a Wikipedia article, or perhaps just asking a friend to write your essay.

One of our webinar speakers, an educator, José Bowen (whose book I reference below), shared his disclosure for students. It's not exactly what you use for an author, but it demonstrates some sort of "risk levels" of AI use.

Template Disclosure Agreement for Students

- I did all of this work on my own without assistance from friends, tools, technology, or AI.
- I did the first draft, but then asked friends/family, AI paraphrase/grammar/plagiarism software to read it and make suggestions. I made the following changes after this help:

- – Fixed spelling and grammar
- – Changed the structure or order
- – Rewrite entire sentences/paragraphs
- I got stuck on problems and used a thesaurus, dictionary, called a friend, went to the help center, used Chegg or other solution provider.
- I used AI/friends/tutor to help me generate ideas.
- I used assistance/tools/AI to do an outline/first draft, which I then edited. (Describe the nature of your contribution.)

And so a publisher could draft something like this for their authors. Let's say the author discloses the top level: I used AI extensively, then edited the results. What then? Do you automatically reject the manuscript? If so, why?

And, meanwhile, if you're paying attention, you learn that that manuscript you just read and loved, which the author swore wasn't even spell-checked by Grammarly, could have in fact been 90% generated by AI, by an author expert at concealing its use.

You're then forced to rethink the question. It becomes, "Why am I so damned determined to detect this thing which is undetectable?"

In part it's the alarmist concern surrounding the copyrightability of AI-generated text. The copyright office won't offer copyright protection to 100% AI-generated text (or music, or images, etc.). But what about 50% AI-generated text? Well, we would only cover the 50% generated by the author. And how would you know which half? We'll get back to you on that one.

Wouldn't it be great if you could just feed each manuscript into some software that would tell you if AI had been used in creating the text?

Leaving aside the issue that the only way to do this would be by employing AI tools, the more important question is, would the software be (sufficiently) accurate? Could I rely on it to tell me if AI had been used in creating a manuscript? And could I depend on it not to produce "false positives"—to indicate that AI had been used, when in fact it had not?

There's now lots of software on the market that tackles these challenges. Many of the academic studies evaluating this software[113] point to its unreliability. AI-generated text slips through. Worse, text that was not generated by an AI is falsely-labeled as having been contaminated.

But book publishers are going to want some kind of safeguards in place. It appears that, at best, these tools could alert you to possible concerns, but you would always need to double check. So perhaps it might alert you to texts that need to be more carefully examined than others? Is this an efficiency?

True efficiency will be found in moving beyond concerns about the genesis of a text, instead maintaining our existing criteria as to the quality of the submitted work.

Job loss

"AI will not replace you. A person using AI will." —Santiago Valdarrama (January, 2023)

Job loss from AI adoption could be severe. Estimates vary widely, but the numbers are grim. There are ob-

vious examples: San Francisco's driverless taxis elim-
inate... taxi and rideshare drivers. AI-supported diag-
nostics reduce the need for medical technicians.

The optimist in me points to, as one example, the introduction of the spreadsheet and its impact on employment. As you see in the chart below, employment in
"Accounting, Tax Preparation, Bookkeeping, and Pay-
roll Services" has nearly doubled since 1990—hardly an
indictment of spreadsheets and other technologies that
have largely automated these tasks.

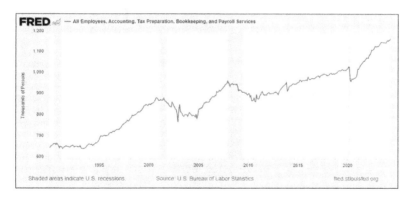

Ethan Mollick's study with the Boston Consulting Group
(BCG)[114] was an experiment that sought to better understand AI's impact on work, especially on complex,
knowledge-intensive tasks. The study involved 758
BCG consultants, randomly assigned to use or not use
OpenAI's GPT-4 for two tasks: creative product innovation and business problem solving. The study mea-
sured the performance, behavior, and attitudes of the
participants, as well as the quality and characteristics
of the AI output.

Among the findings was that "AI works as a skill leveler. The consultants who scored the worst when we assessed them at the start of the experiment had the biggest jump in their performance, 43%, when they got to use AI. The top consultants still got a boost, but less of one." The full article is revealing, and as with all of Mollick's work, provocative yet accessible.

Education

Education has been front-and-center in the pro and con debates about AI. The introduction of AI into classrooms is largely seen as a curse, or at least a challenge. Other educators, like PW's keynoter Ethan Mollick, embrace AI as a remarkable new tool for educators; Mollick insists that his students work with ChatGPT.

The best book on the topic is *Teaching with AI*[115]*: A Practical Guide to a New Era of Human Learning* by José Antonio Bowen and C. Edward Watson.

I'm not going to delve into educational publishing in this book—it's a vast topic, demanding a separate report. Arguably publishing is becoming of secondary interest within education: AI tools are software, not content, per se. Or, stated another way, has software become content?

The future of search

 Search is a fraught topic in AI. I encourage you to visit perplexity.ai[116] to get a glimpse into where things are headed. The next couple of times you're thinking of starting a Google search head over to Perplexity instead.

Perplexity goes a step beyond search links, rephrasing the information it gathers from multiple sources so that you *really* don't have to click a link. It provides links to its sources, but clicking them is unnecessary—you've already got the answer to your question.

Google has moved in the same direction with its "AI Overviews." After Perplexity, return to Google search and type in the same query, and compare Google's AI summary to Perplexity's. It won't be as good.

This seemingly modest shift has huge implications for every company and every product that relies, at least in part, on being discovered through search engines. If searchers are no longer being sent to your site, how can you engage them and convert them to customers? Simple answer, you can't.

More information is available in this report from Bain[117], "Goodbye Clicks, Hello AI: Zero-Click Search Redefines Marketing."

It's still early days for AI and the transformation of search. Stay tuned.

Junk books on Amazon

 AI-generated junk books on Amazon are a problem, though their severity may be more visceral than literal. On the one hand these books are spamming the online bookstore with low-quality and plagiarized content, sometimes using the names of real authors to deceive customers and take advantage of their reputations. The books are not only a nuisance for readers but also a threat for authors, potentially depriving them of hard-earned royalties. AI-generated books also affect the ranking and visibility of real books and authors on Amazon's site, as they compete for the same keywords, categories, and reviews.

Amazon now requires authors to disclose details of their use of AI in creating their books[118]. No doubt this can be abused.

Try searching on Amazon for "AI-generated books."

There are lots. Some of the results are how-to books about the use of AI for creating books. But others are, unabashedly, AI-generated. "Funny and Cute cat images-You are can't see this types of photos in the world-PART-1[119]" (stet) is credited to Rajasekar Kasi. There are no details of his (?) bio on an author page, but six other titles are credited to the name. The book, published August 26, 2023, has no reviews and no sales rank. The ungrammatical title of the ebook doesn't match the ungrammatical title on the cover of the print book.

But other authors are clearly using AI extensively in the creation of their books, and not disclosing. As I discuss above, detecting AI use is next-to-impossible with skilled 'forgers.' Coloring books, journals, travel books and cookbooks are being generated with AI tools in a fraction of the time and effort of traditional publishing.

Search "korean vegan cookbook" and you'll find the top title, "The Korean Vegan Cookbook: Reflections and Recipes from Omma's Kitchen," by Joanne Lee Molinaro, in first place. But trailing not far behind it are other titles that are obvious rip-offs. "The Korean Vegan Cookbook: Simple and Delicious Traditional and Modern Recipes for Korean Cuisine Lovers" has two reviews, including one that notes "This is not a vegan cookbook. All the recipes have meat and eggs ingredients." But the book is #5,869,771 in sales rank, versus the original, which stands at #2,852 on the list.

It's difficult to determine the extent of the harm caused.

Amazon has policies in place that allow it to remove any book that fails to "provide a positive customer experience." Kindle content guidelines forbid "descriptive content meant to mislead customers or that doesn't accurately represent the content of the book." They can also block "content that's typically disappointing to customers." It is the sheer volume that defeats Amazon's watchers? Or is there another reason?

Bias and Deepfake Images

LLMs are trained on that which has already been published online, and on books obtained from pirates. What has already been published is rife with bias, and so LLMs reflect that bias. And of course not just bias, but hate, reflected in its learnings, and now a potential output in AI-generated words and images. Porn is another natural beneficiary of the AI's remarkable facility with images, and there are recent troubling stories of young women finding fabricated nude images, their male classmates as likely suspects. *The New York Times* reported separately about an increase in online images of child sexual abuse.

Authors and publishers need to be aware of these built-in limitations when using AI tools.

Creativity can be a Cliché

 The question of whether machines can be truly creative remains a topic of heated debate. It depends in part on how we define creativity.

"AI will never be creative." That's a familiar mantra.

We all know what creativity is, don't we?

Cambridge: "the ability to produce or use original and unusual ideas."

Britannica: "the ability to make or otherwise bring into existence something new, whether a new solution to a problem, a new method or device, or a new artistic object or form."

I don't dispute that creativity, in this sense, is well beyond the reach of LLMs.

But I argue that most of what's passed off as creative—and often appears quite creative—is, in fact, iterative. Which works perfectly well for many things, including most advertising.

But to raise the 'creativity' stanchion, and then diminish LLMs, is to set an impossibly high barrier, at which AI invariably fails. Then people dismiss AI as "well, I told you it's not creative."

And thereby miss the iterative stuff that it's very good at.

I'll be posting a long essay on this topic in the not distant future, after I finish reading:

The Creativity Code[120], by Marcus du Sautoy, and

The Artist in the Machine[121], by Athur I. Miller

and re-reading *Literary Theory for Robots*[122], by Dennis Yi Tenen

Sentient Creatures

Jeremiah Owyang is an industry analyst (and investor) based in Silicon Valley. He's an AI booster, but he's been around hype before.

As he puts it[123], small teams of programmers now can use LLMs to assemble "sentient creatures"—like a 4-year-old—in two days. They are capable of:

- 'Seeing' with computer vision, what's happening in the real world,
- 'Hearing' via voice commands and ambient sounds in the real world,
- 'Thinking' through processing the above real-world input,
- 'Learning' by accessing the pre-trained data,
- 'Referencing' exclusive data sets,
- 'Speaking' with life-like audio voices, that have inflection and tone in any language,
- 'Writing' through text communication, in any format or style required,
- 'Drawing' by creating images spontaneously, and
- 'Interacting': it can proactively engage in dialog, ask questions, or assign AI agents to complete tasks on their own.

Owyang continues: "I've been in Silicon Valley for 27 years, and have experienced five waves... Friends: I've. Never. Seen. Such. Rapid. Evolution. In. Such. A. Short. Time.

"It's very clear that AI is evolving faster than a humans can, this is exponential capabilities in such as short time."

Will it matter to publishing? You decide.

Essay:
The Impact of AI on the Book Publishing Industry

In this book I've generally considered AI's short-term impact on book publishing. That's evolution. But is a revolution in the offing?

You'll recall Doc Searls' quotation from the introduction to this book: "The next revolution will catch us all off guard, as they always do. Said another way: if the crowd is anticipating the revolution, it can't be the revolution."

By that statement I would likely fail if my prediction was for an incipient AI revolution. Nonetheless, I want to play with the possibility over the next 20 pages or so.

What got me started was a 2023 conversation with Peter Brantley[124], my partner in the AI webinar weeds, about how we might shape upcoming AI programs. Peter works much of the time within the library community, and had just returned from a in-person day-long event in Los Angeles with some 150 of his library colleagues, where they explored AI's potential impact on their sector. The conversation was lively and in-depth. Why, he wondered, don't trade book publishers have gatherings like this? AI is *a* topic at every publishing event: why isn't it *the topic*?

The real-world consequences of AI

The answer Peter came up with is that trade book publishers haven't yet concluded that AI is going to have any **real-world consequences** on their business. On the core of their business. On their ability to conduct business. Sure, it might help write a press release or pen a manuscript rejection letter, but they assume that publishing will still putter along as it's been doing for decades, with the average time from contract to print book dragging on for up to two years.

At the same time, publishers of course face near-term challenges more pressing than AI. Paper prices. Shipping costs. Shrinking margins. Sales mostly flat overall. With all of those pressures, who has the time or bandwidth to care about AI?

But the other creative industries get it. Art[125] and design[126] gets it. Advertising gets it[127]. Hollywood sees what's coming[128], as does the music industry[129]. Journalists are watching with dread[130].

Other book publishing sectors are starting to get a handle on AI's impact. Scholarly publishing is deep into the[131] technology. But trade publishers are acting like there will be few real-world consequences from AI.

What might these consequences be? Will they impact the supply of books? Or the demand for books?

Supply: Yes, AI is the culprit behind a bunch of new garbage books on Amazon. Hundreds? Certainly. Thousands? Probably. Millions? No. How many books are available on Amazon in all formats? More than 50 million. It's very crowded already.

That aside, it's clear that in the near term AI isn't going to be writing *whole* books that people will actually want to read. Its value thus far is as a writing buddy—critiquing, suggesting, occasionally spinning out a few paragraphs of usable text. No, in the near term, AI is not going to be radically changing the outputs of book publishing, the supply of new books.

Demand: No one is demanding AI-generated books. That's not a factor. And I can't foresee any scenario where AI will impact the demand for books more broadly.

What about the process of publishing? Yes, that will change. Publishers are now looking to AI for help here and there: marketing, editorial, a bit of this and a bit of that.

Is it possible that there will be few real-world consequences of AI on trade book publishing? Perhaps it's just a toy[132].

So let's step back from the AI weeds and revisit the troubled state of trade publishing, and through that, drill down into where AI might have its greatest impact.

Publishing has been in economic decline for decades

By varying estimates, the entire book publishing industry in the United States has annual sales of under $35 billion. Apple Computer's annual sales are more than 10 times higher. Apple's gross profit is some 47% of sales, alongside net profits of 24% of sales. Publishing doesn't even dare dream of margins like these.

Trade book publishing has been in a gentle economic decline for decades, some years up a few percent, some years down—overall, trade book publishing is not a growth industry.

In 2024, according to AAP's StatShot[133] "trade revenues were up nearly 5%, at $8.578 billion for the calendar year." An up year, after a decline of 0.3% in 2023.

Without the growth of alternative formats, ebooks and audiobooks, the industry might be in very bad shape. Ebooks were a growth engine for years[134]. Audiobook sales continue to climb. The latest data (as of May 2025) shows sales up nearly 15% in 2022[135] and another 9% in 2023[136]. Yes, some of that is substitution sales, but a lot of the customers for ebooks and audiobooks are new customers, not necessarily regular book readers. In 2024, ebooks and audiobooks accounted for over a quarter of trade sales. Would all of those customers buy print books if print was all that was available?

Retail pricing is becoming an increasing concern as costs and resale discounts squeeze publisher margins. Academic studies suggest that there is a degree of price elasticity for books[137], but surely we're reaching a resistance point: hardcover bestsellers are running up against what may be a $35 price ceiling. "Subscription fatigue"[138] is causing video-on-demand customers to drop services, focused on the increasing cost of each. Netflix's Premium plan now runs to $24.99/month[139]; the Disney Plus Duo Premium is $19.99/month[140]. As a colleague recently remarked to me, how many cash-strapped subscribers will say, oh, let's cancel our Netflix subscription so that we can buy a book next month?

Book publishing salaries

I'm not going to beat this to death: it's not only authors who scramble to make a living—publishing personnel are grossly underpaid compared to other white-collar professions.

I keep a representative smorgasbord of recent publishing job postings. I'm looking at one, for a Marketing Manager at a trade publisher that reported 2024 sales of just over $30 million. The position pays between $60,000 and $70,000 per annum. Here's another, for a Publicity Manager at one of the imprints of a publisher reporting $750 million in annual sales. "This role will have an annual salary of $74,000–$79,000," the listing notes.

According to the U.S. Bureau of Labor Statistics National Occupational Employment and Wage Estimates[141], marketing managers earn, in the mean, across all industries, $166,410. The mean earnings for "Public Relations Managers" are $159,420.

Book publishing isn't even in the ballpark. This is not news to anyone working in publishing. It's always been this way. But can publishing sustain itself at these pay levels? An inability to offer candidates even half of the pay standard does not auger well for an industry growing increasingly digital.

In an age of TikTok, YouTube, social media, SEO, metadata, and author platforms, what the heck is a "publicity manager" anyway?

The three (and-a-half) remaining advantages for traditional book publishers

Three persistent advantages for traditional book publishers are (i) cachet, (ii) access to major media, and (iii) access to bookstore distribution. This doesn't apply equally to all traditional publishers—the largest ones have more of each: more cachet, better access to major media, and better opportunities for getting their books onto the front tables at the largest number of bookstores. But, taken together, these are the characteristic advantages of the traditional book publishing industry.

One other value that publishers sometimes offer is a curated list of complementary titles, where each single title benefits from its companions. Think of a publisher like Fox Chapel[142], specializing in books about crafts: if you enjoy one of their titles, there's a reasonable chance you'll look closely at their other books (and magazines) on the same topic, even if they're written by other authors.

This crosses over to something that only a few publishers have managed to develop, a marketable brand. Think of series like Wiley's "For Dummies," or Oxford's "Very Short Introductions." The brand conveys a consistency of editorial approach and quality that encourages readers to buy multiple titles. Self-publishers often launch their own short series, mostly for fiction, though they can't inhabit the breadth of these larger publisher catalogs.

All of the other services that traditional publishers provide can be purchased on the open market, with similar quality, at affordable prices (for example, editorial, design, production and essential marketing functions). And, for self-publishers, the per-book-sold income is five times or more greater than traditional royalty schedules.

Let me quickly demean the value of the top three advantages. Cachet is good for bragging rights, but has little cash value. Book reviews, and other major media exposure, which have always been tough to get, now have a vastly diminished impact on book sales. And bookstores represent roughly 15% of industry sales (and far less for self-published authors)—they are no longer core to a book's success.

Things have changed.

Self-publishing

Self-publishing has been the main driver of growth in consumer (trade) publishing for the last decade and more. Because Amazon is demure, accurate sales data around self-publishing remains hidden—it's easy to ignore its importance. But the available data shows[143] that self-publishing claims a substantial portion of the trade publishing market.

As Kobo CEO Michael Tamblyn (somewhat) famously noted[144], "One in 4 books we sell in English is a self-published title, which means that effectively, for us, self-publishing is like having a whole other Penguin Random House sitting out in the market that no one sees. It's like the dark matter of publishing." (Penguin Random House's 2024 worldwide sales were just over $5 billion; U.S. sales were $3.2 billion.)

The trends within the self-publishing market are arguably the only significant trends in trade publishing—self-published authors are showing the way. They are adventurous and uninhibited by the customs of the traditional industry. As an example, traditional publishers still shy away from using AI for audiobooks. Self-published authors show no such reservations.

Many are fluent with social media. They are close to their readers, their customers. If you want to learn the latest marketing techniques, follow author forums[145], blogs[146], and newsletters[147].

Dig deep into author income stats, the economics of writing, and then compare the income decline of traditionally-published authors[148] against the income gains of self-published authors. In an international survey and report that I conducted with Steve Sieck[149] for ALLi[150], in 2023 (pdf[151]), we discovered that "the median writing and self-publishing-related income in 2022 of all self-publishers responding was $12,749, *a 53% increase* (italics mine) over the previous year. Average (mean) incomes skewed much higher: $82,600 in 2022, a 34% increase."

Does that sound high? In a separate survey[152], conducted by Peter Hildick-Smith[153] for the Authors Guild in 2023, "full-time self-published authors, who had been publishing since at least 2018, reported a mean income of $24,000 compared to $13,700 in 2018, *a 76 percent increase* (italics mine)."

Hybrid publishers

In part for the sake of thoroughness, I want also to mention hybrid publishers[154], who combine the freedom of self-publishing with some of the rigor of traditional publishing.

It can be expensive, but I've become increasingly enthusiastic about the hybrid model, and the hybrid publishing segment is significant and growing. No one estimates hybrid sales separately. But the impact is most clearly seen in its dominance of two categories: book by celebrities, and in popular business books. These categories have long been reliable income sources for trade publishers, but hybrid publishers' "concierge services," and much more favorable income sharing, are irresistible for many high-profile authors.

Recent developments, like Authors Equity's profit sharing relationship with its authors[155], and Keila Shaheen's 50/50 profit sharing with Simon & Schuster[156], suggest a trend toward the normalization of the hybrid model. This is good news for authors; less promising for traditional publishers.

Publishing beyond publishers

If AI is to transform book publishing, it's going to have to move beyond the book.

I'm co-authoring a report with Rüdiger Wischenbart, based on his original study "Publishing Beyond Publishers[157]." We're trying to understand, and to quantify, as best we can, all of the book-ish publishing activity, worldwide, that could (and should) be included as part of a more comprehensive view of the modern publishing ecosphere.

Once you move beyond the bookish container you find glimpses of where AI could really make an impact.

The poster child for our project is Wattpad, where "97 million people spend over 23 billion minutes a month engaged in original stories." The stories are experienced online, mostly on smartphones, in short chunks. Few become published books. They are just as likely to find their way into "Wattpad WEBTOON Studios, the company's TV, film, and publishing counterparts."

Younger readers are more attuned to online digital reading than their more senior brethren. According to a January 2024 Wattpad survey[158], "digital formats are increasingly popular among younger generations, with 65% of Gen Z and 71% of Millennials embracing webnovels, ebooks and webcomics, while less than half of the Gen X and Boomer generations say the same."

And, of course, as the traditional publishing industry is now learning: "Diversity is a key driver for embracing digital formats: 61% of Gen Z and 70% of Millennials agree that ebooks, webnovels, and webcomics give them access to content that's harder to find in bookstores and libraries, including LGBTQ+ and minority-focused content."

Wattpad has competitors[159]. Several are nonprofit and open source. Inkitt is the top commercial competitor, which, according to *Publishers Weekly*, recently raised $37 million[160] from investors "including Stefan von Holtzbrinck, the owner of Holtzbrinck Publishing Group, which owns Macmillan, and former Penguin CEO Michael Lynton; it has now pulled in a total of $117 million in investment. In February 2023, the *Financial Times* said[161] that Inkitt was the eighth fastest-growing company in Europe, and #1 in Germany." A July 9 article in *Esquire*[162] outlined Inkitt's use of AI, its role in their success.

How many of you have even heard of Inkitt, visited its publishing platform[163], or downloaded its Galatea reading app[164]?

But our "Publishing Beyond Publishers" report goes beyond online story platforms to consider how "content can be created and disseminated in a diversity of formats (print, digital, media (books, audio, movies, games, distribution channels (communities, platforms, streams and business models (sales of products, subscriptions, streaming, freemium, paid models in mostly digitally-defined supply and marketing chains." How many opportunities are book publishers missing because they're not an obvious fit within the current business model?

Innovation, technology and book publishing

With the exception of ebooks, modern publishing has never faced a serious threat from technology. Bookish apps appeared to be potentially disruptive, but only briefly. The dawn of the Internet era offered publishers more opportunity than threat; it's just a single retailer, Amazon, enabled by the Internet, that truly upset the apple cart.

I've never seen a study on whether Amazon has been

(when all aspects of its operations and impact are fully factored) a net positive for the book publishing industry. It reaches many buyers who aren't served by bricks and mortar, and is willing to sacrifice margin to keep prices low. Ebooks and audiobooks are delivered at scale. But Amazon is able to cut prices in part because it demands high discounts and fees from suppliers, and it chokes other retail channels. There are painful trade-offs.

Still, don't try criticizing Amazon in front of a self-published author. They would not be in business without The Everything Store[165].

The innovator's dilemma

To gain a perspective on AI's coming impact on book publishing I recommend Clayton Christensen's *The Innovator's Dilemma: When New Technologies Cause Great Firms to Fail*[166], first published in 1997 by Harvard Business Review Press.

Christensen looks at how existing (incumbent) firms can succumb to the forces of innovation.

Successful, well-managed companies often fail when disruptive changes come to their industry. Conventional management practices, which had helped them to become industry leaders, make it difficult for these companies to be nimble in confronting the disruptive technologies that could cannibalize their markets.

They ignore the products spawned by disruptive technologies, because, at first blush, they compare poorly to their existing products. Their most profitable customers generally can't use the purported innovations and don't want them. Companies try to fight off disruptive threats by doubling down on existing products and services.

Christensen's key insight is that by doing the apparently 'right' thing, including listening to customers, successful companies leave themselves wide-open to disruptive innovation. They focus on their current customers and ignore important new technologies—which initially target small, less profitable markets. It creates an opening for agile startups to disrupt the industry leaders.

Chris Dixon, in discussing the book[167], points out that "the reason big new things sneak by incumbents is that the next big thing always starts out being dismissed as a 'toy.'" Hmm, yes, a lot of people see Chat AI as a toy[168].

Are publishers failing to recognize that innovations built with generative AI might disrupt their fragile business model?

Fiction versus nonfiction

AI's impact on book publishing will have a dramatically different impact on the authoring and publishing of nonfiction than it will on the authoring and publishing of fiction.

The book publishing industry isn't often enough analyzed as two bifurcated industries, one that publishes fiction books and another than publishes nonfiction.

While most trade publishers offer both fiction and nonfiction titles, the industry-wide gulf between the two forms is stark both in the number of titles published, and in book sales. Fiction titles represent roughly 10% of books published each year. Sales, however, greatly favor fiction. There are year-to-year shifts, but fiction captures up to half of annual trade book sales. In 2024, none of the top 10 bestsellers were nonfiction[169]. Using Wikipedia's compilation[170], 84% of the books in English that have ever sold 20 million copies or more are fiction titles.

Book sales trends are notoriously fickle, but fiction sales appear to be on a continuing upward slope. After cratering at 32% in 2019, they claimed 40% of the adult market in 2022.

While AI is going to be increasingly used by fiction authors to aid in the process of creation, as discussed elsewhere, there seems little likelihood that AI-generated stories will take over the bestseller shelves. "Good-enough" AI-generated genre fiction is conceivable, but again not something that should give authors and publishers sleepless nights.

The writing and publishing of nonfiction, on the other hand, will be aided and abetted by AI across the board. It's happening already. Nonfiction authors are taking advantage of Chat AI's many talents both as a research assistant and a writing aid. And nonfiction publishers will increasingly call upon Chat AI for help in manuscript development, fact-checking, editing, marketing and distribution.

When a reader approaches a work of nonfiction the book has no idea who they are. Perhaps they're a high school dropout; perhaps a PhD. They might be brand new to the subject, or maybe just boning up. The "killer app" for nonfiction publishing dwells near here. Chat

AI can customize text to your particular needs and deliver it rapidly, as an ebook or an audiobook, in 200 languages. Print does not compete. Print does not compute.

Is there an existential threat to authors?

I spoke to a very smart author's agent, who has been thinking a lot about what AI means to her clients, and to all professional authors. The conversation turned to the idea of the book as a 'container,' and I asked her to expand on that idea. Her response:

"The basic idea is that when authors/agents are placing a book with a publisher, it is just that: a book. There is an understanding that it might later become one of the myriad forms of derivative works we have come to know (translation, dramatic adaptation, graphic novel, etc.) but all of that is secondary to the 'the Work' itself. The Work is not a bag of words or phrases or facts, it is something structured by the author in a way unique to that author. Breaking the container, shaking the Scrabble bag of letters and drawing out a random selection (that is not entirely random because it is a Scrabble bag made up of the syntax and semantics and style of the specific author), is not what is being considered when we make a grant of rights to a publisher.

"The book is the integral whole that is greater than the sum of its parts. It's the product of a creative epiphany (and a ton of creative intellectual work) that brought it all together as a book, not just 'a' book, but the book by that particular author."

Books contain treasures

When I think about nonfiction books, breaking the container is one of the upsides of the AI era. You break the container, and like Fabergé eggs, there are treasures contained within.

The constraints of the container are both a feature and a drawback. On the one hand "the work is not just a bag of words or phrases or facts, it is something structured by the author in a way unique to that author." On the other hand, in creating the container, the author, by dint of the inherent limitations of the bookish container, was forced to reduce, reject, rewrite, and reconfigure. The work is polished, but it is distilled. Some things were lost (while others were gained) along the way.

People fail to read long nonfiction books all the way through, in part because they've become conditioned to skimming all the text they encounter on the web—even in their emails. The "book summary" model fails for the same reason—instead of an indigestible 250-page nonfiction book you get an indigestible 12-page summary of the book.

Books are like lunch boxes—all the stuff in one place. But I just want the cookies.

It's not going to be easy for established authors to throw off their chains. But they may have to learn to do so, or risk being overshadowed by a new generation of skilled researchers and writers who can express themselves with or without formal containers, as the occasion calls for. Rigid containers impose far too many limits, and limitations.

What it comes down to is that the business of writing has irredeemably changed. It's like the end of the scribes. In this case, our monkish authors must get out from behind their desks and their containerized view of the book, and engage with form and with their audiences.

Oh yes, I know well the author rejoinders: But I'm a writer, I'm not a promoter. I'm not on social media. I don't have a platform. I speak to my readers via occasional interviews and ever-more-occasional appearances. I have a website (but, truth be told, I never update it). My work is my gift to readers. They can accept my work, or reject my work, but I will not be joining them in their living rooms.

Well, you can put away the scrolls and the ink made from the blood of ermines. The occupation of 'author' now demands that you get out from behind your desk and meet your readers where they live, in their living rooms, and on their Facebook pages. You can lament it all you want, as we curtail your grants and your tenure and your publishing opportunities. This is the brave new world of writers and readers, *sans* publishers, those dreadful intermediaries who work hard to enhance and to market your work, yet constantly interrupt the direct connection to your readers, the people who most value your work.

None of this precludes great narrative nonfiction books reaching an attuned audience. *Au contraire.* Those books can continue to shine. Look at the recent Pulitzer Prize nonfiction winners[171]. No one wants publishing to lose its ability to incubate books of this exceptional quality. That would be tragedy. The current publishing business model doesn't need to disappear for the new model to thrive.

I think of these great nonfiction books as 'beautiful.' 'Beautiful' as in beautifully-written, carefully edited, designed with care and deliberation, and printed, with deckled edges, on FSC-certified paper. They are sold in boutiques.

The boutiques are called 'bookstores,' but they have all the characteristics of boutique retail—lovely objects, chosen with care by the owner and the managers, a bit pricey, but for those who treasure such objects, well worth the cost.

The task of most nonfiction authors is now to move beyond the container, as well as the publisher as gate-keeper.

Content containers in multiple media

The reading public, particularly its younger members, is increasingly 'media-agnostic.' In search of entertainment or knowledge, they can be watching a YouTube or TikTok video, a Netflix series, listening on Spotify, scrolling through Instagram ("Insta"), catching up on the news, or, occasionally, reading a book.

Yet the business models are still focused on the unique container. The publishing industry. The film industry. The television industry. The music industry.

Movies are not books. YouTube videos are not movies. Podcasts are not audiobooks.

These silos were not an historical inevitability but a result of a series of technology and business decisions made by powerful organizations over time.

It's not hard to disrupt a business model built upon a single container.

For all of its facility with language, the current generation of generative AI works its magic with even more bravado producing sounds, images and video. AI affords this book with audiobooks, in multiple languages, alongside the 31 translations of the ebook. None of this would be even remotely possible without AI—the economics of traditional production makes no sense for me.

Creative silos

Content creators are traditionally trained to excel in just a single container silo. We have writing programs and film programs and music programs. It rarely occurs to us that creative writers might also take a 'minor' in film or music. Or in computer programming or in app development.

Whatever happened to transmedia[172]? Where are the programs that teach creatives to be, as Apple once framed it, "Masters of Digital Media"?

The best content will always win. But, over time, the content containers matter less and less. The digital generation may not be entirely container-agnostic. But they are container-flexible. They encounter most of their content digitally, via smartphones. Print will continue to find an audience, but it will never again command the center.

The "publisher of the future" needs also to be container-flexible. Most of the growth in content distribution is not via ink on paper, nor words in EPUB files. The growth of audiobooks is no accident, nor is the popularity of YouTube and TikTok.

The larger challenge lies in the necessity of making new and existing content discoverable, whatever its form, and then upon discovery, to turn awareness into a purchase decision.

Discovery and conversion

The online discovery problem has been with us for some time; AI did not create it. The problem is one that industry veteran Mike Shatzkin highlighted more than once[173]. There are so many titles available in print, and digital formats allow them to remain continuously in print. Millions of out of print books can be found from used book retailers. On top of that two million or more new books are published each year, just in English. AI will make the saturation problem worse, but it's already out of hand.

Amazon's algorithms are not selfless—they do a very good job of surfacing what's saleable, the book that you're most likely to purchase next. That book isn't characterized merely by its sales figures. It sold best not because some scammer optimized the online listing. It sold best because it *was* the best, and delighted readers told others to buy it, both online and in person. (Amazon encourages advertising that distort its algorithms, part of the enshittification[174] of the platform.)

I talked above about metadata. Conversion is as vexing as discovery. Can AI help authors turn browsers into buyers?

The future of copyright

The concept of copyright has been fundamentally challenged by developments in artificial intelligence. It's not that authors and other creatives don't want or deserve protection for their work—arguably they deserve it more than ever. And it's not that AI renders copyright unenforceable (at least in some form, if not in the current form).

It's that the "protection of copyright" can also become a veil behind which your work disappears. If your book cannot be at least referenced via a conversation with Chat AI then it, in essence, does not exist on that platform. Why bother protecting that which cannot be found?

This is where the discovery problem might become a catastrophe. Google does a great job discovering books only through their metadata. Omnivorous AI prefers the whole enchilada. Unlike traditional search engines, AI rarely responds to user queries based only on the abstract metadata about a work.

At the same time, evolving content containers, containers other than whole books, suggest different kinds of copyright challenges. If the text of a book can change on the fly, in response to reader input, what then is the copyright of the text? And how can the original author be fairly compensated?

Writers & readers

Publishers need authors; authors don't need publishers.

The future of publishing is the intimate relationship between writers & readers. It's far stronger than the relationship between writers and publishers and readers and publishers. Publishers can be a roadblock in the relationship between writers & readers. In many cases they do not enable the relationship; they impede it.

For a long time, the only way to access high-quality written content was through books or via a modest selection of periodicals. That's certainly no longer the case. Quite apart from the distractions of other media, there are now so many different ways to access (non-containerized) high-quality written content. Books no longer hold the primacy they once enjoyed.

AI can communicate

"What's the perfect book for me to read next?" Generative AI can answer that question with an eloquence and a precision that has never before been possible. As AI becomes a reliable recommender engine, authors will need to communicate via that engine. (Amazon, of course, is working on this,[175] and has the benefit of knowing what you've previously purchased.)

Conclusion

So where does this leave us?

I felt it necessary to catalog the challenges that publishing faces. Chat AI is arriving at a time when trade publishing is troubled. It's not arriving at a time when the industry is robust, and able to say: "we don't need some newfangled technology; we're doing just fine."

I talked above about the most pressing challenges publishing faces: rising costs and shrinking margins.

The wolves will never be sated in their demands for ever steeper discounts; margins will not improve. Retail prices are near a ceiling. The future of the current trade publishing model lies in cost reduction.

Salaries cannot go any lower, so we'll need to cut costs within the production cycle.

But publishers have been trying to cut production costs for decades. There have been some notable successes, but we've exhausted the current options.

I've shown that AI can bring efficiencies to publishing, across the workflow. They're not instant and they're not easy: you need to work at AI. But the opportunity is there.

Publishers are not looking to reduce staffing, so the objective has to be more books coming more quickly to market based on current staff resources. AI tools can further that objective.

And, of course, there's always a goal of selling more

copies of the books being published. AI can help there as well.

My simple recommendation to publishers is to employ AI tools with the objective of driving 15% out of fixed costs, while seeking a 15% increase in backlist sales, in any format.

I describe above how AI can be transformative to the longer-term future of publishing as well.

Don't worry about that. Get your house in order, and we'll talk further.

Some Additional Sources

There is now a near-endless supply of material available to help inform you on AI; far too much, of course. Choose your preferred medium: books, blogs, newsletters, videos, podcasts, courses and psychic divination. I've linked to some key sources through this book—it's worth clicking a few random links in the ebook to see where they take you.

There's only one excellent AI book for literate beginners, Ethan Mollick's Co-Intelligence[176], which was released in April 2024. It's drawn from his equally excellent (free) newsletter, "One Useful Thing[177]."

My 7-part AI webinar series[178], co-produced with the Book Industry Study Group (BISG), features some topic-focused content on a range of AI & publishing issues and opportunities.

George Walkley offers a free newsletter[179]for publishers that covers AI news.

Joanna Penn's Patreon[180] contains a treasure trove of information about practical AI (and some other topics), focused more on authors than on publishers, but useful for both.

Side Note:
Credentials for Writing This Book

I didn't want to burden the introduction with this information, but I know that people are skeptical of the folks writing about AI today, suspicious that many of these authors are fashioning themselves as latter-day AI experts. No doubt some are. I hope that I have acceptable credentials to undertake this project.

I read my first book about artificial intelligence in 1988, a book published two years previously, *Understanding Computers and Cognition: A New Foundation for Design*[181] by Terry Winograd and Fernando Flores. The book is dense—much of it was beyond my understanding—but it was the first time I got excited about the possibilities of artificial intelligence in book publishing.

By that time I was deep into the weeds of the digitization of publishing, occasioned by the explosion of desktop publishing, Apple computers, PageMaker and the like. I continued to work in publishing technology, as a consultant and analyst, working with some of the leading software and hardware vendors, including Adobe, Apple and Microsoft. I also became involved with, and a part-owner, of a software company called Enfocus. We created an automated system for prepress workflows.

We didn't have access to AI at that juncture, but we got very good at unleashing fully automated publishing production systems. As AI can be indistinguishable from magic, so too can the best of automation appear to resemble AI.

Fast forward to 2016, and my colleague Cliff Guren helped me focus on AI in book publishing[182]: it was beginning to look like something was finally happening. *The Bestseller Code*[183] (Archer and Jockers) appeared in September, 2016, making it clear that computers could interpret the texture of literature with a high degree of insight and precision.

By that time I was paying close attention to book publishing startups[184], and a small number emerged with some degree of AI technology wound into their software offerings.

Fast forward again, to October 2022.

A month before the release of ChatGPT, and several months before Chat AI became the topic everyone in publishing was talking about, Tim O'Reilly presented to the PageBreak Conference[185] on "AI and Publishing Transformation." O'Reilly is well-known in the publishing community, both for O'Reilly Media and for the Tools of Change conference. He's one of tech's top visionaries.

O'Reilly was not merely enthusiastic about the new advances in AI, he was over the top. "We're at a point that's very similar to how I felt when we discovered the Worldwide Web in 1992," he said, and followed that with "this is as transformative as VisiCalc, the PC, and the web browser."

He admitted that the use case was still fuzzy, pointing to a couple of pilot projects at O'Reilly Media. But, he said, "this is getting better scarily fast. Machine learning is not a future thing anymore. This is about the democratization of AI."

O'Reilly talked about how publishers should approach these new technologies, saying that they need to "know when to burn the boats and go all in. There's a time when you have to commit."

PageBreak was the first publishing conference to put AI front and center, via Tim's insights.

Disclosures

This book has five sponsors. I knew when writing the book that there would be few riches to be found, and I decided to underwrite my efforts by inviting sponsors to participate.

As I indicate on my website[186], working as a consultant, an analyst, and as a journalist, I support the International Federation of Journalists' Global Charter of Ethics for Journalists[187]. Paragraph 13 is clear on the obligation to avoid conflicts of interest or "any confusion between (my) activity and that of advertising or propaganda."

Having sponsors suggests a conflict of interest and a confusion around advertising. If I was working for the *New York Times* it would be simple: "No." Working for myself, disclosure is my weapon to satisfy these obligations: I'll describe the consideration I've received and you can judge, in my work, if I have been compromised.

I chose the sponsors that I invited to this project because I was familiar not only with their work but with the individuals involved in their organizations. They include colleagues and friends. I told them that their products might be discussed in the text of this book and they would have no control over those words. What they could control was their advertisements at the end of the book—I would post those as supplied. That's what I've done.

I have received payments from others that may have influenced my work on this book—I can catalog the following:

- I have not done any paid consulting work for the AI vendors described in this book, including the sponsors.
- I received some profit-sharing revenue from *Publishers Weekly* for the AI webinars in September, 2023 and from BISG for our monthly webinar series.
- I'm paid a standard per word rate for my *Publishers Weekly* articles.

Please let me know if you detect any favoritism that you think may have resulted from these engagements. My broad bias in favor of AI was formed early.

About the Author

Thad McIlroy is a publishing technology analyst and author, and principal of The Future of Publishing[188], based in San Francisco. He is a contributing editor to *Publishers Weekly*, covering artificial intelligence, digital innovation and publishing startups. His latest book, *The AI Revolution in Book Publishing: A Concise Guide to Navigating Artificial Intelligence for Writers and Publishers*, was first published in July 2024, revised in May 2025.

McIlroy has authored a dozen books and over five hundred articles on digital publishing. He is co-author of the industry-standard *The Metadata Handbook, 2nd Ed*[189] (co-authored with Renee Register). McIlroy served for five years as Program Director for Seybold Seminars, the publishing industry's premier technology conference.

He is a founding partner in Publishing Technology Partners[190], a consultancy focused on the broad range of strategic technology issues in publishing.

An expert on publication metadata and online book marketing, he has taught the Metadata for Books course at Pace University in New York, in their Masters of Publishing Program. In 2024 he joined the advisory board of Johns Hopkins University Press and became a visiting scholar at the Publishing Master of Professional Studies program at The George Washington University. He is a Senior Member of the Association for Computing Machinery (ACM).

Acknowledgements

I wouldn't be able to discuss AI with any credibility if it weren't for the support of *Publishers Weekly*, including the editor emeritus, Jim Milliot, and the former CEO & Publisher, Cevin Bryerman. Jim supported my early writing about AI, and Cevin (alongside Krista Rafanello and the rest of the team) were instrumental in the success of the fall 2023 conference, *AI and the Revolution in Book Publishing*[191].

And further thanks to numerous colleagues...

- Peter Brantley, for all of your help in getting my head around AI and publishing.
- Cliff Guren, long-time sparring partner, sometime co-writer, and insightful reader of the drafts of this book and other projects.
- Two other 'beta' version readers offered valuable feedback: Joe Wikert and Brad Farmer.
- Hannah Johnson, many thanks for the cover design.
- My Publishing Technology Partners[192], Ken Brooks, Bill Kasdorf, Bill Rosenblatt, Bill Trippe, Steve Sieck, and our newest associates, Lettie Conrad and Linda Secondari and Maja Thomas.
- My sister, Anne Pashley, who helps me keep the publishing startup database current, and constantly energizes my research efforts.
- Bill Kasdorf helped me drill down on the accessibility issues for this book.

- Peter Armstrong and Len Epp at Leanpub were patient with my questions and quibbles and helped me through the process of offering the best possible outcome for the book on the Leanpub platform.
- Hugo Rayne at ElevenLabs for audiobook support.
- My good friend and reliable detector of my writing and reasoning foibles, Bob McArthur.
- I wouldn't have returned to San Francisco and dug into generative AI if it weren't for the encouragement of my long-time friend Zach Stewart at the Canessa Printing Company and Gallery[193].

Sponsors

BOOK ADVISORS LLC
Transaction services and consulting for publishers

David Lamb and **Susan Reich** formed Book Advisors LLC in 2016 to consult on mergers and acquisitions in publishing. We have completed more than a dozen transactions, as well as a variety of financial, distribution, and operational consulting projects, including fair market valuations. We are pleased to have recently worked in association with **Clarke & Esposito**; **Thad McIlroy** of The Future of Publishing; and **Kuo-Yu Liang** of Ku Worldwide.

We pride ourselves on our relationships, diligence, and discretion. Whether you are interested in buying, selling, financing, or consulting, please get in touch for a confidential discussion.

bookadvisorsllc.com | bookadvisors@gmail.com

PAPERCUTZ

has been acquired by

Mad Cave Studios

August 2022

In association with Ku Worldwide LLC

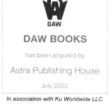

DAW BOOKS

has been acquired by

Astra Publishing House

July 2022

In association with Ku Worldwide LLC

CASLON PUBLISHING

has been acquired by

Brookes Publishing Co.

April 2022

In association with Thad McIlroy

B.E.S. PUBLISHING

has been acquired by

Sourcebooks

November 2021

APPLEWOOD BOOKS

has been acquired by

Arcadia Publishing

April 2023

EREWHON BOOKS

has been acquired by

Kensington Publishing

October 2022

Firebrand Technologies is a software and service company that has been assisting book publishers with data and workflow management solutions for more than 35 years.

NetGalley is an online platform that connects publishers and authors to reviewers, librarians, booksellers, media, and educators who discover new books on Net-Galley and recommend them to their audiences.

As developers of software and digital solutions, Firebrand Technologies and NetGalley are also industry experts and active members of the publishing community. Our solutions benefit all aspects of the publishing process, from acquisitions all the way to sales and marketing.

- **NetGalley**[194] helps publishers build buzz for titles, receive quick feedback and reviews, and discover early trends.
- **Title Management Enterprise**[195], along with its' compact version, **Title Management Lite**[196], is Firebrand's core software application that provides advanced publishing workflow

management throughout the entire publishing process.

- **Eloquence on Demand**[197] is the publishing industry's most powerful ONIX distribution platform, distributing metadata and digital assets to over 600 trading partners in ONIX and other formats.
- **Flywheel**[198] is a backlist marketing service that identifies hidden opportunities in the backlist for increased discoverability and sales.
- **Eloquence on Alert**[199] monitors live title data and trends in the marketplace and alerts publishers of critical mistakes and opportunities that can impact sales (missing buy buttons, third party sellers, etc.).
- **FlightDeck**[200] is the most advanced EPUB Validation and Testing tool available.

Perfect Bound

The marketplace connecting publishers with printers around the world.

Welcome to a better way to print books.

Perfect Bound was created in 2022 to help address the supply-chain issues that have been plaguing the book publishing industry for years. Periods of excess capacity at printers are followed by short windows of delays due to supply crunches. Perfect Bound seeks to open up the printing market to independent publishers and authors by allowing printers from all around the globe to easily connect and do business with publishers looking for new and dynamic suppliers.

What is Perfect Bound?

Perfect Bound is a two-sided marketplace that connects independent book publishers with printers in the U.S., Canada, Colombia, Brazil, Turkey, China, Malaysia, India, and more.

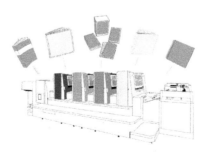

Discover new publishing partners with one click

Our robust platform allows you to simply build out product quotes, send out requests to hundreds of printers with the click of a button, negotiate and finalize your print runs and track products from the press to the warehouse. As a printer, connecting with new publishers, bidding on upcoming projects and getting paid has never been easier or more secure.

Connect with new publishing partners instantaneously

- Send and receive print requests from around the world
- Execute and track print runs from the press to the warehouse
- Transact seamlessly using ACH payments through Stripe without leaving the platform

perfectbound.io[201]

Automated advertising that sells books

Shimmr drives higher book sales, by creating and deploying automated, end-to-end advertising that continuously self-optimizes.

Monetization of catalogs for Publishers

Awareness, reach and recognition for Authors

Discovery of new and more fulfilling books for Readers

shimmr.ai

All in a simple monthly subscription

Unlocking potential through special interests

Can she survive the alley's dangers?

A new level unlocked: The world of AI awaits

Make your setbacks into comebacks: Adaptability and resilience

Scan the code to book a demo

hello@shimmr.ai

www.shimmr.ai

Meet Insight, an AI platform built specifically for publishers

"Adopting Insight for our publishing house was like swapping a bicycle for a Ferrari. Suddenly, everything moves faster."

—-German children's book publisher and Insight customer

Work Smarter, Achieve More

Developed by Veristage, Insight empowers publishers to thrive in the evolving AI landscape. Using AI and a robust suite of digital tools, Insight analyzes and understands your documents and books, in order to help you:

- **Create, improve, and refresh** metadata

- **Speed up** the creation of title-specific marketing, publicity, and sales materials
- **Identify and evaluate** a book's key messages, unique selling points, target audience, comp titles, and more
- **Optimize** your marketing and sales content for maximum reach, engagement, and increased sales

Unlike generic AI platforms, Insight is engineered to function within publishing workflows and to help you create publishing-specific information and assets.

How It Works

1. Upload your book to the Insight platform
2. Insight's AI tools analyze and understand your book
3. In a few minutes, Insight generates a wide range of metadata and key information about your book for editorial, marketing, publicity, sales, and rights departments
4. Enter manual edits to any of this information directly in the platform. Your book and AI content is saved within Insight, so you can access it anytime.
5. Use our document-aware AI Chat to optimize your title information, interact with your books, and incorporate book details into communications and other materials

Security and Copyright

The Veristage team is committed to providing AI services that are secure and protect publishers' intellectual property. Our platform has advanced information security systems in place, and we only work with AI models that do not store or use your data to train future models.

Solutions for Publishers of All Sizes

Insight is designed to work for publishers of all shapes and sizes, from consumer to academic, from three-person teams to multinational organizations. We offer competitive pricing and scalable solutions.

Talk to us to find out how Insight can benefit your business:

www.veristage.com[202]

Notes

1 https://link.springer.com/article/10.1007/s12109-019-09665-5

2 https://leanpub.com/authors

3 https://www.tandfonline.com/doi/full/10.1080/10494820.2019.1674887

4 https://www.publishersweekly.com/pw/by-topic/industry-news/trade-shows-events/article/94820-bisg-looks-to-the-future-at-annual-meeting.html

5 https://www.booknetcanada.ca/blog/2018/1/19/what-it-means-to-be-accessible

6 https://www.w3.org/TR/epub-a11y-11/

7 https://www.w3.org/WAI/tutorials/images/

8 https://chatgpt.com/

9 https://claude.ai/

10 https://copilot.microsoft.com/

11 https://gemini.google.com/app

12 https://www.nytimes.com/2024/04/02/podcasts/transcript-ezra-klein-interviews-ethan-mollick.html

13 https://www.linkedin.com/pulse/co-intelligence-living-working-ai-ethan-mollick-alex-kasavin-2gqbf/

14 https://www.penguinrandomhouse.com/books/741805/co-intelligence-by-ethan-mollick/

15 https://ourworldindata.org/brief-history-of-ai

16 https://www.technologyreview.com/2024/03/04/1089403/large-language-models-amazing-but-nobody-knows-why/

17 https://www.mckinsey.com/featured-insights/mckinsey-explainers/whats-the-future-of-ai

18 https://www.gartner.com/en/topics/generative-ai

19 https://www.futurepedia.io/resources/ai-fundamentals

20 https://www.linkedin.com/pulse/how-does-ai-really-translate-revisiting-chinese-room-pedchenko-32hne/

21 https://arstechnica.com/science/2023/07/a-jargon-free-explanation-of-how-ai-large-language-models-work/

22 https://answers.microsoft.com/en-us/msoffice/forum/all/what-is-the-percentage-of-features-of-word-excel/80e417ef-8336-49a5-9f5f-0a59c8c8fbd4

23 https://dictionary.cambridge.org/us/dictionary/english/idiot-savant

24 https://openai.com/index/chatgpt-plus/

25 https://guides.lib.montana.edu/ai/prompt

26 https://www.ibm.com/think/topics/prompt-engineering-guide

27 https://www.nytimes.com/2024/04/11/technology/personaltech/ai-pin-humane-openai-microsoft.html

28 https://www.youtube.com/watch?v=jhdxGn3APn0

29 https://openai.com/index/sora/

30 https://deepmind.google/technologies/veo/veo-2/

31 https://thefutureofpublishing.com/2024/08/ai-a-story-in-video/

32 https://www.publishersweekly.com/pw/by-topic/digital/content-and-e-books/article/95034-book-business-ai-showcase-shimmr-and-pix.html

33 https://leanpub.com/translate_word/buy

34 https://www.deepl.com/en/products/translator

35 https://leanpub.com/translate_ai/buy

36 https://www.salesforce.com/artificial-intelligence/

37 https://www.oracle.com/artificial-intelligence/

38 https://www.knkpublishingsoftware.com/white-paper-ai/

39 https://www.virtusales.com/biblio-ai-lab

40 https://www.klopotek.com/klopotek-publishing-radio

41 https://www.linkedin.com/posts/klopotek_ai-artificialintelligence-customerservice-activity-7161284409353027584-AHYN/

42 https://www.klopotek.com/post/ai-metadata-and-machine-learning-in-publishing-optimizing-discoverability

43 https://www.supadu.com/

44 https://cdn.prod.website-files.com/5f64854a08f25a50068763b1/65d4803da5c760712be6160d_NEW%20Smart%20Intelligence%20AI%20-%20A5.pdf

45 https://www.publishersweekly.com/pw/by-topic/industry-news/publisher-news/article/90959-book-publishing-startups-in-the-u-s-2022.html

46 https://publishers.org/news/publishers-submit-reply-comments-to-copyright-office-in-artificial-intelligence-proceeding/

47 https://www.publishers.org.uk/trade-bodies-issue-joint-statement-on-artificial-intelligence/

48 https://www.independentpublishersguild.com/IPG/Latest/Blogs/IPG/Posts/AI-in-publishing--where-we-are-and-what-s-coming-next.aspx

49 https://www.independentpublishersguild.com/IPG/IPG/Events/Training.aspx?hkey=28d1e75d-f573-4fdc-b303-2407823815f2

50 https://www.georgewalkley.com/

51 https://docs.google.com/document/d/1qlZ-INPqzWdrPl_hPUVMpEV5NrCx5dcmrAuicGBu-5c/edit#heading=h.8bpuf0ittcnb

52 https://www.bisg.org/workflow-committee

53 https://www.thebookseller.com/features/publishers-outline-ai-practices-in-attempt-to-balance-efficiency-and-creativity

54 https://www.bertelsmann.com/news-and-media/news/new-study-on-ai-in-the-media-industry.jsp

55 https://lunch.publishersmarketplace.com/2024/04/prh-develops-generative-ai-tool-for-employees/

56 https://www.publishersweekly.com/pw/by-topic/industry-news/trade-shows-events/article/95102-u-s-book-show-book-biz-ceos-discuss-navigating-rapid-changes.html

57 https://newsbreaks.infotoday.com/NewsBreaks/The-US-Book-Show-2024-Artificial-Intelligence-Audiobooks-and-Movie-Deals-164304.asp

58 https://perfectbound.co/page/ai

59 https://en.wikipedia.org/wiki/TeX

60 https://en.wikipedia.org/wiki/Standard_Generalized_Markup_Language

61 https://coko.foundation/

62 https://www.robotscooking.com/ketty-ai/

63 https://www.robotscooking.com/redefining-document-design-unveiling-our-ai-powered-pdf-designer/

64 https://blog.adobe.com/en/publish/2024/04/23/the-future-pro-design-generative-ai-taking-off-indesign

65 https://www.hurix.com/how-ai-is-revolutionizing-indesign-workflows/

66 https://integranxt.com/ai-ml-solutions/

67 https://veristage.com/insight-product-features/#support-marketing-and-sales

68 https://search.worldcat.org/title/968758718

69 https://www.ingramcontent.com/retailers/metadata-essentials

70 https://publishdrive.com/publishing-assistant-metadata-generator.html

71 https://veristage.com/insight-product-features/#support-marketing-and-sales

72 https://www.editeur.org/files/ONIX%203/APPNOTE%20Aspects%20of%20AI%20in%20ONIX.pdf

73 https://www.digital-science.com/tldr/article/dark-matter-whats-missing-from-publishers-policies-on-ai-generative-writing/

74 https://www.oreilly.com/terms/ai-policy-for-talent.html

75 https://www.elsevier.com/about/policies-and-standards

76 https://www.nytimes.com/2024/04/10/business/investment-banking-jobs-artificial-intelligence.html

77 https://pdxscholar.library.pdx.edu/eng_bookpubpaper/39/

78 https://www.publishersweekly.com/pw/by-topic/industry-news/publisher-news/article/87762-ai-comes-to-audiobooks.html

79 https://about.fb.com/news/2023/11/decade-of-advancing-ai-through-open-research/

80 https://hotsheetpub.com/2024/01/audible-filling-with-ai-narrated-books/

81 https://www.publishersweekly.com/pw/by-topic/digital/content-and-e-books/article/97756-audible-expands-catalog-with-ai-narration-and-translation-services.html

82 https://www.youtube.com/watch?v=IMwm8NBmycI

83 https://sudowrite.com/

84 https://futurefictionacademy.com/

85 https://www.nytimes.com/2024/04/12/podcasts/transcript-ezra-klein-interviews-dario-amodei.html

86 https://www.anthropic.com/news/anthropics-responsible-scaling-policy

87 https://www.theatlantic.com/technology/archive/2023/09/books3-database-generative-ai-training-copyright-infringement/675363/

88 https://aicopyright.substack.com/p/the-books-used-to-train-llms

89 https://www.bakerlaw.com/services/artificial-intelligence-ai/case-tracker-artificial-intelligence-copyrights-and-class-actions/

90 https://chatgptiseatingtheworld.com/2024/09/01/status-of-all-30-copyright-lawsuits-v-ai-no-trial-judge-bibas-invites-renewed-summary-judgment-motions/

91 https://www.federalregister.gov/documents/2023/03/16/2023-05321/copyright-registration-guidance-works-containing-material-generated-by-artificial-intelligence

92 https://www.infodocket.com/2024/07/31/u-s-copyright-office-releases-part-1-of-artificial-intelligence-report-recommends-federal-digital-replica-law/

93 https://www.nytimes.com/2024/01/25/technology/ai-copyright-office-law.html

94 https://en.wikipedia.org/wiki/Authors_Guild,_Inc._v._Google,_Inc.

95 https://www.storywise.ai/

96 https://astrolabe.aidanmoher.com/angry-robot-ai-publishing-storywise/

97 https://x.com/angryrobotbooks/status/1777392566121501093

98 https://web.archive.org/web/20230808191400/https://blog.shaxpir.com/prosecraft-linguistics-for-literature-8721473c753b?gi=43a9b0b854d0

99 https://www.wired.com/story/prosecraft-backlash-writers-ai/

100 https://www2.societyofauthors.org/2023/06/07/artificial-intelligence-practical-steps-for-members/

101 https://www.prorata.ai/

102 https://www.createdbyhumans.ai/

103 https://www.copyright.com/media-press-releases/ccc-pioneers-collective-licensing-solution-for-content-usage-in-internal-ai-systems/

104 https://www.publishersweekly.com/pw/by-topic/digital/copyright/article/95512-ccc-launches-collective-licensing-for-ai.html

105 https://www.publishersweekly.com/pw/by-topic/digital/copyright/article/95512-ccc-launches-collective-licensing-for-ai.html

106 https://www.grammarly.com/ai-writing-assistant

107 https://www.grammarly.com/business/learn/enterprise-grade-generative-ai/

108 https://otter.ai/

109 https://insider.microsoft365.com/en-us/blog/transcribe-comes-to-word-for-windows

110 https://authorsguild.org/resource/ai-best-practices-for-authors/

111 https://www.bisg.org/events/can-ai-be-detected-in-writing

112 https://mailchi.mp/hotsheetpub/how-publishers-sell-books#mctoc3

113 https://arxiv.org/abs/2403.19148

114 https://www.oneusefulthing.org/p/centaurs-and-cyborgs-on-the-jagged

115 https://www.press.jhu.edu/books/title/53869/teaching-ai

116 https://www.perplexity.ai/

117 https://www.bain.com/insights/goodbye-clicks-hello-ai-zero-click-search-redefines-marketing/

118 https://kdp.amazon.com/en_US/help/topic/G200672390#aicontent

119 https://www.amazon.com/Funny-images-You-types-photos-world-PART-1-ebook/dp/B0CGQ9W9NM

120 https://www.hup.harvard.edu/books/9780674244719

121 https://mitpress.mit.edu/9780262539623/the-artist-in-the-machine/

122 https://wwnorton.com/books/literary-theory-for-robots

123 https://web-strategist.com/blog/2023/11/30/one-year-openai-has-evolved-faster-than-a-human-child/

124 https://www.linkedin.com/in/naypinya/

125 https://nhsjs.com/2023/the-future-of-ai-art-and-its-potential-interactions-with-the-art-industry/

126 https://webflow.com/blog/how-ai-will-transform-design-systems

127 https://www.ft.com/content/0ac1fe79-4c2a-4030-8046-061293ba1127

128 https://variety.com/2023/digital/features/hollywood-ai-crisis-atificial-intelligence-eliminate-acting-jobs-1235697167/

129 https://www.newyorker.com/magazine/2024/02/05/inside-the-music-industrys-high-stakes-ai-experiments

130 https://www.newyorker.com/news/the-weekend-essay/is-the-media-prepared-for-an-extinction-level-event

131 https://scholarlykitchen.sspnet.org/2023/01/18/guest-post-ai-and-scholarly-publishing-a-view-from-three-experts/

132 https://cdixon.org/2010/01/03/the-next-big-thing-will-start-out-looking-like-a-toy

133 https://publishers.org/news/aap-december-2024-statshot-report-overall-publishing-industry-up-6-5-year-to-date-and-down-4-3-for-month-of-december/

134 https://www.publishersweekly.com/pw/by-topic/industry-news/bea/article/57390-bea-2013-the-e-book-boom-years.html

135 https://publishers.org/news/aap-december-2023-statshot-report-overall-publishing-industry-up-0-4-for-calendar-year-2023-and-down-2-5-for-month-of-december/

136 https://www.publishersweekly.com/pw/by-topic/industry-news/audio-books/article/95187-u-s-audiobook-sales-hit-2-billion-in-2024.html

137 https://link.springer.com/article/10.1007/bf03396924

138 https://civicscience.com/one-subscription-too-many-video-streaming-reaches-an-inflection-point-as-consumers-report-feeling-subscription-fatigue/

139 https://help.netflix.com/en/node/24926

140 https://www.disneyplus.com/

141 https://www.bls.gov/oes/

142 https://lancasteronline.com/business/local_business/fox-chapel-publishing-plans-4-million-expansion/article_64cfdbd4-ccb0-11ec-972b-5bc8db28f00c.html

143 https://porteranderson.com/2015/06/15/how-big-is-self-publishing-data-dancing-on-the-platforms/

144 https://www.publishersweekly.com/pw/by-topic/international/Frankfurt-Book-Fair/article/90670-frankfurt-book-fair-2022-global-50-ceo-talk.html

145 https://absolutewrite.com/forums/index.php

146 https://www.thecreativepenn.com/blog/

147 https://hotsheetpub.com/

148 https://www.publishersweekly.com/pw/by-topic/industry-news/publisher-news/article/93301-author-incomes-post-small-gains.html

149 https://www.linkedin.com/in/stevesieck/

150 https://www.allianceindependentauthors.org/facts/

151 https://www.allianceindependentauthors.org/wp-content/uploads/2023/06/The-Independent-Author-Income-Survey-updated-FINAL-17-04-23.pdf

152 https://authorsguild.org/news/key-takeaways-from-2023-author-income-survey/#:~:text=Full%2Dtime%20self%2Dpublished%20authors%20who%20had%20been%20publishing%20since,2018%2C%20a%2076%20percent%20increase.

153 https://authorsguild.org/news/ag-panel-explores-drop-in-authors-earnings/

154 https://www.ibpa-online.org/page/hybridpublisher

155 https://www.publishersweekly.com/pw/by-topic/industry-news/publisher-news/article/94507-three-publishing-veterans-form-a-new-house-authors-equity.html

156 https://www.nytimes.com/2024/05/30/books/booksupdate/keila-shaheen-shadow-work-journal-tiktok.html

157 https://www.wischenbart.com/product/publishing-beyond-publishers/

158 https://company.wattpad.com/blog/the-future-of-fiction-wattpad-research-reveals-generational-shift-in-reading-habits-skepticism-of-ai-in-publishingnbsp

159 https://www.similarweb.com/website/wattpad.com/competitors/

160 https://www.publishersweekly.com/pw/by-topic/international/international-book-news/article/94456-inkitt-nets-another-37-million-for-ai-powered-publishing.html

161 https://www.ft.com/ft1000-2023

162 https://www.esquire.com/entertainment/books/a61485201/books-ai-lawsuits/

163 https://www.inkitt.com/

164 https://apps.apple.com/us/app/galatea-novels-audiobooks/id1380362212

165 https://www.nytimes.com/2013/10/29/books/the-everything-store-jeff-bezos-and-the-age-of-amazon.html

166 https://store.hbr.org/product/the-innovator-s-dilemma-with-a-new-foreword-when-new-technologies-cause-great-firms-to-fail/10706?sku=10706E-KND-ENG

167 https://cdixon.org/2010/01/03/the-next-big-thing-will-start-out-looking-like-a-toy

168 https://www.theatlantic.com/technology/archive/2022/12/chatgpt-openai-artificial-intelligence-writing-ethics/672386/

169 https://www.publishersweekly.com/pw/by-topic/industry-news/bookselling/article/94047-women-ruled-the-2023-bestseller-list

170 https://en.wikipedia.org/wiki/List_of_best-selling_books

171 https://www.pulitzer.org/prize-winners-by-category/223

172 https://henryjenkins.org/blog/2007/03/transmedia_storytelling_101.html

173 https://idealog.com/?s=discovery

174 https://en.wikipedia.org/wiki/Enshittification

175 https://www.theverge.com/2023/12/13/23999804/amazon-your-books-library-recommendations

176 https://www.penguinrandomhouse.com/books/741805/co-intelligence-by-ethan-mollick/

177 https://www.oneusefulthing.org/

178 https://www.youtube.com/playlist?list=PL_yl6l18-hIsnJyVYQcYholPOzZXn3odP

179 https://www.georgewalkley.com/newsletter/

180 https://www.patreon.com/thecreativepenn

181 https://books.google.com/books/about/Understanding_
Computers_and_Cognition.html?id=2sRC8vcDYNEC

182 https://thefutureofpublishing.com/2016/12/publishing-turning-
into-2017/

183 https://us.macmillan.com/books/9781250088284/
thebestsellercode

184 https://thefutureofpublishing.com/2022/11/an-authoritative-
look-at-book-publishing-startups/

185 https://pagebreakconf.com/schedule2022/

186 https://thefutureofpublishing.com/business/the-future-of-
publishing-consultant/

187 https://www.ifj.org/who/rules-and-policy/global-charter-of-
ethics-for-journalists

188 https://thefutureofpublishing.com/

189 https://search.worldcat.org/title/968758718

190 https://pubtechpartners.com/

191 https://www.youtube.com/watch?v=vknSz_-rNtc&ab_channel=
publisherswkly

192 https://pubtechpartners.com/

193 http://www.canessa.org/office-space.html

194 https://netgalley.com

195 https://firebrandtech.com/solutions/title-management/

196 https://firebrandtech.com/solutions/title-management-lite/

197 https://firebrandtech.com/solutions/eloquence/

198 https://unlockyourbacklist.com/

199 https://eloquenceonalert.com/

200 http://ebookflightdeck.com/

201 https://perfectbound.io/

202 https://veristage.com/about/#contact